CUSTOMER SERVICE:
the cornerstone of success

*winning strategies, philosophies,
and practices*

by
Rene A. Henry

© 2013 Gollywobbler Productions

LIBRARY OF CONGRESS CATALOGING-IN-PUBLICATION DATA

Henry, Rene A. (1933-   )
    Customer Service: the cornerstone of success
    Rene A. Henry – 1st ed.
            p.   cm.
    Includes biographical references and index
    ISBN# 978-0-9674535-5-2
    1. Customer service. 2. Business. 3. Public Relations
    4. Marketing 5. Sales
    I. Title

Library of Congress Control Number: 2012950688

© 2013, Rene A. Henry
Gollywobbler Productions
1474 21st Avenue
Seattle, Washington 98122

www.renehenry.com
Cover design by Jack Cullimore
Jack Cullimore Graphic Design, Ilwaco, Washington

First Edition, 2013
10 9 8 7 6 5 4 3 2 1
Printed in the United States of America

Other Books by Rene A. Henry

The Iron Indians, the story of the incredible 1953 William & Mary football team, Gollywobbler Productions, 2011

Communicating In A Crisis, a guide for management, Gollywobbler Productions, 2008

Offsides! Fred Wyant's Provocative Look Inside the National Football League, Gollywobbler Productions and Xlibris, 2001

You'd Better Have A Hose If You Want To Put Out the Fire, the complete guide to crisis and risk communications, Gollywobbler Productions, 2001

Bears Handbook – Stories, Stats and Stuff About Baylor University Football, co-author with Mike Bishop, Midwest Sports Publishing, 1996

Marketing Public Relations – the HOWs that make it work!, Iowa State University Press/Blackwell Wiley Publishing, hardcover 1995, paperback 2000

MIUS and You – The Developer Looks At A New Utility Concept, co-author with Joseph J. Honick, Fernando Oaxaca and Richard O'Neill, U.S. Department of Housing & Urban Development, 1980

How To Profitably Buy & Sell Land, John Wiley & Sons, 1997

Table of Contents

PART I

The Basics

Chapter I

Introduction

A customer is the most important visitor on our premises. He is not dependent on us. We are dependent on him. He is not an interrupter of our work, but the purpose of it. He is not an outsider to our business. – Gandhi

Well done is better than well said. – Benjamin Franklin

Many companies, organizations and institutions boast about their customer service but, unfortunately, at so many it is simply only rhetoric. For years customer service has been on the decline not only because a new generation of customers neither expects nor demands great service, but because so many CEOs today don't understand how to deliver great service.

In many businesses customer service is an oxymoron. In many others it is an overused buzz word. It is a shame that the Federal Trade Commission cannot sanction, fine and reprimand for mis-representations, false and misleading advertising those who falsely boast of being the best in customer service.

When I think of customer service names that come to the top of my list and excel are Alaska Airlines, Amazon, Amica Mutual Insurance Co., Corniche Travel, Crystal Cruise Lines, Fidelity,

1

Hampton Inns, Marriott, and Nordstrom. Doing business with each of these companies is a pleasure.

There undoubtedly are other companies who provide extraordinary customer service that could be added to my list, but those I have named are only those with whom I have had a personal, first-hand experience. To list the worst would require a several set volume of books!

Years ago I could have added a score of names to my list. Regrettably, new management with a different philosophy does not consider customer service a priority and many of these businesses now live on their past reputation.

Don't always believe the companies that advertise and boast they are number one in customer service are indeed the best. The companies that provide outstanding customer service don't need to brag or advertise about it – they just deliver. Their satisfied customers keep returning and telling others. The story of extraordinary service gets told by word-of-mouth.

No Magic To Doing It Right

There is no magic to customer service. It is basically just good old fashioned common sense, being courteous and polite, and making a little extra effort to please a customer. It is how you want to be treated when you are spending money for a product or service. Those providing customer service should treat everyone the way they would want to be treated, only better. Nonprofit, for profit, and government organizations all need to provide customer service.

The basic principles of customer service work equally as well for the mom-and-pop store, neighborhood market and local dry cleaner as for a *Fortune 500* company.

"Studies show strong customer service pays great dividends to an organization's long-term stability and growth," writes Chris M. Martin, a contributor to eHow.[1] She believes a key indicator of quality customer service is customer loyalty and it relieves pressure to attract new customers. "Statistics show it costs more to get new customers than it does to retain existing ones."

Martin says the typical customer will talk to people more about negative customer service than a positive experience. "The typical customer will tell between eight and 25 people about a negative experience and Internet postings will continue to magnify the complaint," she says. "However a typical customer will only tell one or two people about a positive experience."

Time and again poor customer service or lack of it has contributed significantly not only to creating, but also exacerbating crises. Customer service should be an integral part of any crisis management and communications plan. Something as simple as not returning a phone call, or not responding to a letter, email, text or fax, not only can lose a sale, an existing or future customer, but can even create a crisis. With the exception of spam, junk mail and robodialed calls, that is why it is important to always respond.

From the CEO to the entry level employee, everyone needs to understand that the customer is one reason they have a job. Employees and executives alike should consider that providing excellent customer service is job insurance. Yet customer service continues to get worse every year.

U.S. Becoming A Rude Society

Being rude has become all too common place in society today. Plain old fashioned common courtesy has disappeared. The United States is not alone. Degrees of rudeness vary in countries throughout the world depending on the culture and customs. I believe the proliferation of social media, combined with new technology, has been a major contributor. Almost everything today is impersonal. Many people are just too quick to quick to click.

"As rudeness is becoming increasingly common in our culture, Americans are finding it more difficult to work with each other," writes Rachel Alexander, editor of the *Intellectual Conservative*. "This self-centered generation has developed an attitude that they are 'entitled' to be rude, entitled to cut each other down. Instead of greeting others with a smile, brightening their day, it has become commonplace to be negative and grouchy towards others, including their co-workers."[2]

Society does change with each new generation. Another answer to rudeness could be defined by Bill Hybels, pastor of Willow Creek Community Church who believes angst, agitation and a troubled sense of soul seem to be endemic in our culture. Located in the Chicago suburb of South Barrington, Illinois, the church is one of the most attended in the country.

On a recent train trip I sat next to a young man and we talked about the problem of our society becoming so rude. He said he and his wife were bringing up their children exactly the way they were raised by their parents. "Friends and neighbors are always complimenting us on the politeness of our children," he told me. "We once thought this was rather unusual but have realized that we are exceptions."

Chivalry is dead. Long gone are the knights in shining armor. Some analysts and psychologists blame the feminist and women's liberation movement. Few men today hold a car door open for a lady and few women expect it. Regardless of gender, few people even hold elevator doors for others and when they do, the beneficiary seldom says "thank you." The words *thank you, please* and *you're welcome* are quickly disappearing from vocabularies.

This is just the way society is today. While many people are inadvertently rude, I do not believe some are intentionally rude. They simply just do not know any better.

All of this has built a culture in opposition to customer service. Few people expect customer service and even fewer demand it. Albert Einstein summed it up years ago when he said: "I fear the day that technology will surpass our human interaction. The world will have a generation of idiots."

Exceed Expectations

"Exceed your customers' expectations. This goes back to the idea of excellent customer service, but it also goes beyond that," says Jim Cabela, vice chairman of Cabela's Incorporated, Sidney, Nebraska outfitters. "Consumers have grown to expect quality customer service. To be successful, you must reach beyond those expectations."[3]

Management needs to empower all of its employees to take ownership of customer service and build a sense of spirit and pride within the company, business and organization. Often it is just the little things that could easily go unnoticed that make a difference. Being polite and cheerful in greeting a customer is important. Some employees will go the extra step and address by customer by name.

I remember when banks did business this way and almost everyone in your local bank welcomed you and even called you by name. I give high marks to my local Madison Park branch office of Wells Fargo which does an extraordinary job and also to my Wells Fargo mortgage broker, Tom Golon, and his team. Golon is the reason I have originated and refinanced my residence with him six times. In 2012 he was voted #1 for customer service in the Seattle Metropolitan Area.

It should be an automatic response and not an effort for sales people to reach out to a customer. You know a salesperson considers customer service a priority when you are physically taken to a particular aisle or location rather than just being pointed in the general direction. Or when a supermarket cashier asks a customer if she or he needs help in getting groceries to the car. The Publix Super Market in Palm Beach, Florida, even provides valet parking for its customers whether they are driving a Rolls Royce, Bentley, Volkswagen or Smart Car.

Excellent customer service translates to the bottom line. The best practitioners in the business can even point to pricing their products and services higher than their competition. The object is to build customer loyalty where customer service is a priority and not price.

Principles Are the Same Regardless of Size

The principles of customer service are the same regardless of size and work equally as well for a small business as for an international conglomerate. A good example is Pete White who has had a successful career in the life insurance business for more than half a century. With his son, Brad, he heads The White Planning Group in Charleston, West Virginia. In 2013 he celebrated his 55 years in the business and his 50th as a member of the Million Dollar Roundtable. He believes in any business the principals need to maintain contact on a regular basis with customers.

"One of the biggest problems in a business today is the lack of service to customers," he says. "Too often you are given an 800 number to call and good luck on getting an answer to your problem. This is particularly true in the financial services industry.[4]

"In my opinion, when you purchase a product or service you are entitled to an answer to your questions. The successful business should have a simple procedure to provide this answer," White adds. "Having someone to contact in the business office is essential to providing customer-oriented service without referring the customer to call an 800 number." He signed his first contract on his 25th birthday, starting in business after serving in the military.

Why Customers Switch Companies

A study by *U.S. News and World Report* said that 68 percent of customers are more likely to leave a product or service for a competitor because of a bad experience.[5]

"Customers want to be loyal but customer service often fails to meet their expectations," says Robert Wollan, global managing director of Accenture Sales & Customer Services. According to the Accenture's 2012 Annual Study on Customer Service, one in five U.S. customers switched companies they buy from, a five percent increase over the year before. Some 85 percent say the companies could have done something different to prevent them from switching. The eighth annual survey covered 10 industries and polled more than 12,000 consumers in 32 countries.

Broken promises are a top area of frustration for consumers according to Accenture, a global management consulting, technology services and outsourcing company. The largest increases in switching were among wireless phone providers, Internet service providers, and retailers.

Two-thirds of the respondents indicated it is extremely frustrating when a company delivers a different customer service experience from what it promised. Another 78 percent said they are likely to switch providers when promises are broken. Other frustrations included having to contact customer service multiple times for the same reason; dealing with unfriendly agents; and being on hold for a long time.[6]

Accenture also found that a tailored experience is critical to a strong customer relationship. Nearly half of those surveyed have higher expectations of getting specialized treatment for being a "good" customer and that it is important for the company to know their history so they don't have to repeat themselves each time they call. "To convince customers to stay and spend more, many companies will need more tailored offers and interactions that connect with consumers' specific needs," said Michelangelo Barbera, managing director for Europe, Africa and Latin America. The industries that ranked highest for providing tailored experiences were travel and tourism, retail banking and life insurance.[7]

The Boss Sets the Example

Leadership for customer service starts at the very top. Harry S Truman said it best: "The buck stops here." Every employee must know the importance of customer service and the boss needs to empower all employees to always act in the best interests of the organization. During the 1980s, Britain's Lord Taylor, with the same philosophy, established a model for customer service and communication that should be a model for all senior executives.

Jim Cabela takes several hours each week to read and respond to letters and e-mails sent to him by customers. His senior managers do likewise. This is probably why the company has become the world's foremost outfitter, and is always ranked among the top in customer service surveys. He also has taken ideas suggested by customers and profitably incorporated them into the business.

"Customer service is definitely the backbone of our business

– a backbone that bends but won't break," says Cabela. "Superior service gives you an edge keeping your customers. Having a superior product is also very important, but without the superior service to back it up, your customers will go someplace else where they can get the same product and that little something extra."[8]

When it comes to customer satisfaction, no CEO did a better job than the late Lord Taylor of Taylor Woodrow, a British conglomerate. The company was involved in everything from building nuclear power plants and the English Channel tunnel, to residential housing developments in the U.K., U.S., Canada and Spain.

At a social function one evening, a friend confronted Lord Taylor about a problem. He was so concerned that he sent an edict to all employees that from that day forward he be sent any customer complaint. Failure to do so would result in immediate termination, whether the employee was a secretary or a division president. Because of his concern and dedication combined with his hands-on management style, he empowered his employees to resolve customer problems and within months complaints virtually disappeared.

Amica Mutual Insurance Company, a 100-year-old property, casualty and life mutual insurance company headquartered in Providence, Rhode Island believes loyal employees create loyal customers. Nearly 30 percent of its employees have been with the company for 20 or more years.[9]

"Satisfied employees lead to satisfied customers. Long- term employees lead to long-term relationships with customers," says Vince Burks, Amica's senior assistant vice president and communications director. "And pride, trust, and morale are all contagious.

"Well-trained, long-term employees know how to get the job done quickly, efficiently, and effectively. They know their customers. They know their colleagues. They know their company. And they therefore know how to 'get to yes' with ease and a sense of grace," Burks adds. "This is good for the customer and this is good for the company."[10]

Carl Sewell, chairman of Sewell Automotive Companies in Dallas, Texas, believes that it requires great people to provide great customer service. "To be the best, we need to find people who are 10s on a scale of one to 10," he says. "I think we are able to attract better people because of the way we treat them.

"Our people are just as important as our customers, and they need to be treated just as well," Sewell continues. "And just as we thank our customers for doing business with us, we thank our employees for doing a good job." He also believes that whenever possible you show your gratitude on company time by having a party at 3 p.m. on a Wednesday rather than on a weekend day or holiday.[11]

Sam Walton, the legendary founder of Walmart, said "There is only one boss. The customer. And he can fire everybody in the company from the chairman on down simply by spending his money somewhere else."

The Nordstrom Way

For years Nordstrom has been a favorite of journalists who write about customer service. The company is even praised by its competitors for its quality of service. There are probably more books on the market about how Nordstrom provides such extraordinary customer service than any other company or business. In fact, Seattle author Robert Spector has written four.

In 1887, John W. Nordstrom emigrated to the U.S. from Sweden. A dozen years later he struck gold in the Klondike Gold Rush and in 1901 partnered with Carl F. Wallin to open a shoe store in Seattle. By 1960 Nordstrom had expanded to eight stores in Washington and Oregon but only sold shoes. Its growth was based on customer service, deep product offerings and a full range of sizes.[12]

In 1963 the company expanded into apparel and today is considered one of only a handful of upscale fashion specialty retailers in the country. Based on its philosophy of providing outstanding customer service and by opening its own new stores rather than by acquiring other retailers, Nordstrom today has 231 stores in 31 states and 52,000 employees.[13]

The company went public in 1971 and is now run by a fourth

generation family of brothers with Blake W., Erik B., and Peter E. Nordstrom in the senior roles.

Nordstrom management empowers its employees with ownership and entrepreneurialism and they all share their experiences with others in the company. The strategy is built around the customer and not price, process, brand, technology or anything else. The one question is "What would the customer want? This creates a long-term sustainable relationship with customers.[14]

New employees are given a 5"x8" card with the employee handbook that reads:

Welcome to Nordstrom

We're glad to have you with our Company. Our number one goal is to provide outstanding customer service. Set both your personal and professional goals high. We have great confidence in your ability to achieve them.

Nordstrom Rules: Rule #1: Use best judgment in all situations. There will be no additional rules.

Please feel free to ask your department manager, store manager or division general manager any question at any time.

Using one's best judgment continues as the #1 policy in all aspects of the job for all employees.[15] The best Nordstrom sales person will do everything possible to make sure that a shopper leaves the store a satisfied customer.[16] I know that from personal experience.

The company has been ranked by *Fortune* magazine as one of "The 100 Best Companies to Work For In America" since the ratings began in 1998. Because of its reputation for excellence, a score of companies have referred to themselves as "The Nordstrom of their industry." Even Blake Nordstrom used this reference when talking about the Rack division of clearance stores: "We like to think that the Rack is the Nordstrom of the discount world."[17]

Nordstrom executives are humble when it comes to talking about how they provide quality customer service. "We know there is always room for us to improve, so we prefer to simply remain focused on doing our best to serve our customers every single day," says Brooke White, vice president of corporate affairs.

Customer Care Means Repeat Business

Sometimes the customer is wrong. In his book, Carl Sewell has one chapter that discusses when the customer isn't always right. "If the customer is unhappy with something we've done, we'll ask him what's wrong and fix it for free. Almost always.

"But is the customer always and absolute right no matter what? No," Sewell adds. He notes exceptions being a question of fairness or the amount of money involved and believes over $500 it becomes a judgment call. He cites examples of where customers claim a tennis racquet, expensive clothing or other items were left in a car and were gone when the car was returned from service. "Can we get cheated?" he questions. "Yes. Do we mind getting cheated a little bit? No. It's the cost of doing business, and we budget accordingly."[18]

Deborah Gardner, president of Compete Better Now!, Phoenix, Arizona, who writes and speaks professionally on customer service, is another person who believes that not everyone will agree that the customer is always right. "Customers may think they are right, but in their heart they know they are not always right," she says. "It's just a matter of a competitive stance by the customer of trying to push your buttons to see what they can get away with. I know, I'm a customer too."

Gardner says to think about all of the time, effort, and money spent into converting prospects into customers. "Once they become your customers, do you think your customers are satisfied? Customer satisfaction doesn't always mean customer loyalty," Gardner says. "These days, even if your customers appear completely satisfied with your product or service, 40 to 50 percent of them will leave you and start doing business with your competition. Today, satisfying the needs of your customers by providing fast, efficient service is no longer enough. You must move beyond customer satisfaction and engage your customers in memorable experiences that are consistent with your brand promise."[19]

During many of her workshops and programs she cites personal experiences including when she was one of the first guests at a new Shamburg Renaissance Hotel in suburban Chicago. "From all of the world traveling I do, I rarely get sick. However, as I approached the front desk, wishing I was home in my own bed, the front desk clerks noticed that I could hardly stand.

"They quickly checked me in and asked if there was anything I needed. Once I was settled in my room, the housekeeper knocked on the door to know if I needed anything at all. The front desk told her that I was not feeling well. Just 20 minutes later, room service arrived with a bowl of hot soup, crackers, a 7-Up, and a get-well card from the chef and staff. I was so impressed with the trail of communication from the front desk to the housekeeper to room service to the chef regarding my situation that I felt much better just because they took notice while serving me.

"Whether it is serving your customers or collaborating in your department, office or team, taking the initiative to own your responsibilities is huge," Gardner adds. "It's up to you to take charge on how the customers are serviced. Do you think I will return to that hotel when in the Chicago area again? You bet I will."[20]

Making An Extra Effort

Another successful executive who went out of his way to please consumers, even if a complaint was not valid, was the legendary Robert Mondavi. In 1966 he founded the winery bearing his name which was the first major winery built in California's Napa Valley in the post-Prohibition era. He had been part of the family-owned Charles Krug Winery but left following an argument with his father and younger brother.

Harvey P. Posert, who was public relations director for Mondavi for 16 years, tells how his boss handled complaints. "The first day I was on the job I received a complaint, and having never handled one before, asked him how he wanted to handle it," says Posert. "Do we replace the bottle?" I asked. Mondavi responded "We send two bottles."

Posert said Mondavi's policy was to please customers even when he knew they were wrong. "Once, a consumer who lived in Virginia sent us what appeared to be a disintegrating fly and claimed it came in a bottle of our wine. We had the remains analyzed at a laboratory at the University of California-Davis," he continued. "The entomologists there told it was an Eastern housefly not seen in California. I forwarded the results to the complainant with two bottles of wine." When companies respond to complaints like Mondavi it says a great deal about the importance placed on customer service.

Mondavi established standards for New World wines by aggressively promoting and labeling wines by variety rather than generically. One of his well-known successes was Opus One, a proprietary Bordeaux-style blend in collaboration with Baron Philippe de Rothschild, considered by wine experts as one of the most outstanding red wines produced in the U.S. at that time. The partners established a $60 retail price for the wine, the highest ever for a California wine. "In each market introduction, Bob would say, 'If any consumer or trade person finds we haven't met our high standards, please return the wine.' The record shows that none were returned," Posert added.

Amazon's Customer-Centric Philosophy

According to Booz Allen Hamilton what distinguishes a customer-centric business from others is that it has moved beyond lip service and re-oriented its entire operating model around the customer, increasing customer satisfaction and profitability in the process.

"Customer-centric companies understand not only what the customer values, but also the value the customer represents to their bottom line," says the management and technology consulting firm.[21]

In July 1994, Jeff Bezos started Amazon in the garage of his Bellevue, Washington home. A year later the company site went online and within two months its sales were $20,000 a week with customers in all 50 states and 45 countries.

With Bezos' philosophy that Amazon's success depended on its customers and it had to make its customers the focus in all stages of its interaction with them, the company today is the world's largest online retailer. In 2012 sales exceeded $61 billion and 51,300 employees were serving customers around the world.[22]

From just selling books, Amazon diversified to selling DVDs, CDs, MP3 downloads, software, toys, electronics, video games, apparel, furniture, jewelry and even home-delivered fresh organic food. Known for his innovativeness, Bezos has taken the company into consumer electronics with the Kindle e-book reader, Kindle Fire tablet computer and now as a major provider of cloud computing services.

Bezos' objective is for Amazon to be the Earth's most customer-centric company. And, it is well on its way with rave reviews and accolades from a broad range of customers. "We sell about 700 books a month that Amazon ships to the buyers," says Bob Frank, founder of RJF books. "Without Amazon handling and shipping and customer service, my wife and I would be running to the post office or someplace every day with dozens of packages."

Praise for Amazon is repeated by a number of authors who have had best-selling books on Kindle. "Amazon and Kindle Direct Publishing are literally enabling creativity in the publishing world and giving writers like me a shot at their dream. For that I am forever grateful," says Blake Crouch.

"The publishing world is changing fast. Writers have more options and readers have more choices," says Theresa Ragan. "Seize the opportunities that KDP offers ... there is zero downside risk and the potential is virtually unlimited," says Robert Bidinotto.[23]

According to Bezos, authors who sell on Kindle can be paid royalties of 70 percent compared to only 17.5 percent on ebooks by the largest traditional publishers. "The KDP royalty structure is completely transformative for authors and good for readers because they not only get lower prices but access to more diversity," he says. "Many of our authors who might have been rejected by establishment publishing channels now get their chance in the marketplace."[24]

Booz Allen Hamilton cites Amazon as perhaps the most visible company using technology to tailor customer life-cycle marketing. It says Amazon uses a customer's past purchases and browsing behavior, as well as the purchases of similar customers, to tailor recommendations to the customer's distinct preferences.[25]

For a number of years I have been both a pleased Amazon customer and author/vendor with books selling both on Amazon.com and Kindle.

Sometimes Pleasing the Customer Can Backfire

There are situations when you do not always want to do what the customer asks. Ritz-Carlton has received numerous honors and awards for being an outstanding hotel chain. The company is proud of its credo where it pledges as its highest mission the care and comfort of its guests. The hotel's computer system keeps a record of what a guest likes including everything from a preference for the way eggs are cooked to the type of sparkling water so any Ritz-Carlton in the chain will be totally prepared when the guest returns.[26]

The hotel chain has learned the hard way that you can't always grant the wishes of every guest. The computer told the staff at the Ritz-Carlton in Naples, Florida that a British couple did not want to be served by "people of color" or "workers with foreign accents." When the couple dined in the hotel's Grill Restaurant on March 10, 2010, this so upset Wadner Tranchant, a restaurant captain and Haitian-American, that he filed a lawsuit for $75,000 damages. A public relations nightmare followed and the Ritz-Carlton has now banned the couple from staying at any of its properties.[27]

A "Can Do" Philosophy

Steelcase, Inc., of Grand Rapids, Michigan is the world's largest manufacturer of office furniture. Paul Witting, who retired as senior vice president of marketing after nearly three decades with the company, attributes a good portion of the success to a customer service "Can Do" philosophy.

"While customer service is an overused word, it plays a major role more than most folks think in the success or lack of success in any company," says Witting. "Naturally there are countless activities and services that go into effective customer service."

All Steelcase products are sold through appointed retail office furniture dealers. The dealers in turn bring the products and services to the end user-customer. "Any time a dealer or customer needed help on a special product or out of the ordinary service, the attitude of the Steelcase person in the position to respond to the request was a positive 'yes, we can do that,'" he adds.

Witting cites an example when he was national sales manager and received a call on Thanksgiving morning from a dealer in Washington, D.C. "The dealer was in the middle of installing a large number of cubical workstations that had to be completed by the following Monday. He forgot to order a few parts necessary to complete the installation and was desperate.

"After getting the information from our dealer, I phoned Bob Hoogterp, the plant manager where the parts needed were manufactured. We both left our families and met at the plant that morning, gathered the parts and put them on a plane that afternoon for next day delivery. The customer moved in on Monday unaware of the crisis," Witting said.[28]

"Bob Hoogterp's attitude that Thanksgiving holiday was no exception. It was a common everyday Steelcase employee response. 'Can Do' is a wonderful ingredient to have in a company culture."

Another important part of the culture exemplified by Witting and his Steelcase colleagues is being available and reachable 24/7.

Fidelity – The Customer First

In 1965 Edward C. "Ned" Johnson III and his father founded Fidelity Investments. Today the company is one of the world's largest and most diversified financial services companies with $3.5 trillion of assets under administration, including managed assets of $1.6 trillion. Fidelity has 40,000 employees serving more than 20 million individuals and institutions.

Johnson's daughter Abigail is now the heir apparent to succeed her father as president and CEO. The Johnson family's philosophy is a commitment to continuous improvement and peerless customer and client service by always putting the customer's interests first. In 2011 the Fidelity Investments was the most honored of 19 brokerage firms for "exceptionally valuable and comprehensive service to customers and prospects in a user-friendly, well-designed interface." Corporate Insight honored the company with seven Gold E-Monitor awards plus silver and a bronze.[29]

Throughout the years I have had my individual and retirement brokerage accounts with more than a dozen different firms – some purely as a result of a merger or acquisition. While I have owned Fidelity mutual funds for many years, since 2006, all of my accounts have had extraordinary and superb service and advise from my Fidelity representative, Timothy Boyle. For the first time I can go to one single website and have a complete picture of my portfolio and all necessary forms to report taxes are easily downloaded.

Airlines Before Deregulation

Before Congress deregulated the airline industry in 1978, airlines competed for customers based on service. Flying was a pleasure. There were no hidden fees or extras as there are today. All passengers had blankets and pillows. All meals, drinks and amenities were free, even in coach class. There were always sufficient quantities of entrees in first class so every passenger could be served his or her choice. Free reading materials included magazines and newspapers. On transcontinental flights between New York and Los Angeles, and before the days of computers, some airlines even had portable typewriters available for passengers.

Large wide body aircraft were configured for first class lounges. The 747 upstairs was a first class lounge. Now these seats are sold and sometimes considered business class on some airlines. Other airlines even had lounges mid-ship on their widebody jets for coach passengers, complete with a piano and popcorn. Pan Am had a lounge area on its 707s where first class passengers could relax before a meal. The purser had a complete bar and would make any drink requested.

When the industry was regulated the government made every effort to ensure that no airline ever went out of business. The airlines spent millions of dollars lobbying Congress for deregulation and after Sen. Howard Cannon (D-Nevada) introduced the Airline Deregulation Act and it became law, many airlines merged or went out of business. Pan Am. TWA. Eastern. Braniff. National. Western. PSA. Piedmont. Allegheny. Ozark. Even no frills discounter People Express shut down its engines. Some 100 smaller airlines went bankrupt or were liquidated.

For passengers, shareholders, employees and retired employees, the industry has since been in a tailspin. Except for a handful of carriers, customer service is not in the vocabulary of most airlines. Legendary comedian Bob Newhart was a visionary when he recorded his 1960s monologue about the Grace L. Ferguson Airline & Storm Door Company. Most of the time when I'm flying, I believe I'm on that airline!

Alaska Airlines – The Culture

Alaska Airlines has won virtually every award and honor given to airlines for on-time performance, customer satisfaction, and frequent flier programs. The Seattle-based airline also is consistently ranked one of the very best in various categories by the travel magazines.

Bradley D. Tilden, president and CEO, attributes this to the company's culture and passion for customer service. "We take extraordinary pride in how we take care of our customers both in safety and service," he says.

"We want our employees to have a mental image of Alaska having just one airplane flying between two cities, not a fleet of 175 planes serving nearly 100 destinations," he adds. "We want our pilots, mechanics, flight crew, agents and all to serve our passengers as if we had only 15 employees and not 10,000, and that everyone's job depends on repeat business from satisfied customers.

"Keeping this in mind, we want our employees to respect and support each other and to work together as a team for the benefit of the customer."[30]

Tilden believes an integral part of Alaska's culture is how the airline's employees have been empowered to use their discretion and best judgment to help and resolve issues with passengers. All flight attendants and agents have an empowerment tool kit complete with vouchers, discounts for future flights, and other amenities that they can use as they wish to handle customer service issues without involving a supervisor.

"Additionally, whenever we have situations such as extreme flight delays, someone from management will quickly be on the scene to help our employees provide whatever is necessary for the comfort of our passengers whether it is bottled water, pizzas or sandwiches. They all have credit cards to use," says Tilden.

Last year he launched a company-wide program called Flight Path that brings together groups of 150 employees across all job levels and disciplines and includes pilots, mechanics, flight attendants, agents, and management. "We got together to listen to our employees talk about the industry landscape and the challenges facing Alaska Airlines, and talk about the actions and the sense of working together that will be required for us to have sustained, strong performance.

"We also look our frequent fliers for their feedback. Periodically we randomly select a few of our best customers and invite them to meet with us over lunch. In addition, every month our senior executives call at least one of our passengers to get their input."

Tilden, who also is a licensed pilot, believes CEOs need to interact as much with front line employees as with management. He frequently walks around various Alaska operations behind counters, down jetways and on the tarmac to get feedback from employees first hand. On Christmas and other holidays he personally thanks the employees who are working. "The risk in any company is that decisions made in the corporate office or board room are not relevant in the field," he says. "How real is what we're working on?

Are our customers and our employees benefitting from our decisions?"[31]

I've been a fan of Alaska since I first flew the airline in the mid 1980s. As both a customer and writer, I've always found all Alaska employees to be very customer-oriented and responsive. Replies to correspondence come from senior management and not come from someone with a pseudo title like "executive correspondence" or "office of the president."

This is a good example of why Alaska Airlines won the J.D. Power and Associates "Customer Satisfaction Award five years in a row. Alaska took top honors in four of the seven categories: check-in, reservation, flight crew, and boarding-deplaning-baggage categories.[32]

The airline has been honored with numerous Freddie Awards, considered the most prestigious consumer-generated honors in the travel industry, for its frequent flier program, best elite level frequent flier program, best frequent flier program website, and best frequent flier program member communications. At one time Alaska's Gold Award when frequent fliers reached certain mileage levels was a one gram chip of 999.99 fine gold. At the time I wish Alaska flew to the destinations where I travelled.

In 2010, 2011, and 2012 Alaska took top honors as the undisputed leader in flight and airport information services and best on-time performance for North America.

Corniche Travel – Service First

When Anastasia Kostoff-Mann started her travel management business many travel companies across the country were closing their doors because the airlines had quit paying commissions.

She attributes her more than 26 years of success to the principles she applied during her days in hotel sales at the Stanford Court in San Francisco and the Beverly Hilton and Beverly Wilshire hotels in Beverly Hills. In the 1970s, she was one of the first women in hotel sales.

"I applied the same principles to travel management, long

before that kind of service was ever heard of at 'travel agencies.' I nixed that 'classification' years ago," she says, "because we are not 'agents' of the airlines but consultants and managers of travel related activities and budgets for the companies and individuals we serve.

"One of the things I brought to the table was tenacity, attention to detail, and an enormous, relentless need to please my customers and clients. Today they call that service.

"I refused to fail and believed that saying 'no' to anyone was to fail. That's the successful philosophy of Corniche Travel and why we remain privately held and operated. We have never had the need – financially or otherwise – to sell or merge. Our independence keeps us free to go the distance."

She cites as an example the time when she overhead a new employee say "no" to a client because she could not clear the flight and hotel room he wanted. "Call him back and tell him that you weren't satisfied, would work further on the flight and hotel room and would call him back," Kostoff-Mann said. "We called our contacts, got everything cleared and my employee's eyes lit up. She was thrilled to call back our client and say 'Yes, now it's done!'

"She told me that when she worked doing travel at American Express she was instructed to get off the phone as quickly as possible and to get on to the next call. I told her to do exactly the opposite at Corniche Travel because we spend as much time as is necessary to get the job done.

"Service is a boundless issue we experience every day," she continued. "American Airlines used to be our #1 preferred provider for many years because of the great way their team took care of us and our clients both in the booking process and in the air. Once they slipped into bankruptcy, everything stopped. The company got rid of some of their best employees and basically eliminated customer service. Now United is on top and, amazingly, Delta is back in our good graces."

She notes that Corniche has never lost a client because of service and the few that have been lost are a result of a merger or acquisition and a new management team. I have been a very pleased Corniche client from day one and always recommend their services.

Corniche Hits A Home Run for the Dodgers

In 1987 and for 20 years Corniche was the travel management company for the Los Angeles Dodgers baseball team and became the team's partner in all things travel, meeting and event related.

"The team contracts for player housing for out-of-town games throughout the season but it never spilled over into the playoffs or the World Series," says Kostoff-Mann. "Each hosting team had this responsibility and it became a nightmare. The team's traveling secretary had little time or backup staff to take on such a difficult project.

"We created a system and were retained by Major League Baseball because they soon saw that the Dodgers were the only team prepared in and on time. We handled all of the teams, all the divisions of MLB and the sponsor groups.

"Just think of asking scores of hotels in a dozen cities to hold hundreds or up to thousands of rooms without a contract or any guarantee and to do so for months on end while certain teams were in contention," she said.

"We worked with Marriott Hotels in most cities because they were baseball savvy and friendly. When others saw the model we created, Hilton and other chains and boutiques and independents started bidding for the business."

Organizing the Customer Service Team

In any company, organization or institution, customer service starts with the boss – the head of the entity. This individual is responsible for setting the standard and determining how high to raise the bar.

A customer service team should be organized and a plan drafted with goals and objectives. The team also needs to periodically review the plan, monitor employees to see if it is working, and survey customers to be sure they are satisfied. It also is important to monitor the competition. Where the customer service department is placed on an organization chart will depend on whether it is in a nonprofit, for-profit or government entity.

In a for-profit business, customer service should be a collaborative effort between sales and public relations. The sales department is responsible for revenues and that means satisfied customers while the public relations department is responsible for the image and reputation of the company or organization.

Carl Sewell disagrees that companies should have a special department or team for customer service. He believes customer service is too important to be left to a "consumer relations" department and that the people who deal with customers must have the authority to resolve problems. "Everybody should be a customer service rep. Let your employees take care of their customers," he says. "Nothing is more important than the customer."[33]

Endnotes

[1] Chris M. Martin, "What Are the Benefits of Good Customer Service?", *eHow*, www.ehow.com.

[2] Rachel Alexander, *Townhall* magazine, September 20, 2012.

[3] David Cabela, *Cabela's – World's Foremost Outfitter – A History*, Paul S. Eriksson, publisher, Forest Dale, Vermont, 2001.

[4] Interview, emails with Pete White, January 2013.

[5] Chris M. Martin, op.cit.

[6] "Consumers Defect in Growing Numbers But Majority Say 'You Could Have Kept Me,' Accenture Research Finds," December 5, 2012, www.accenture.com.

[7] Ibid.

[8] David Cabela, *Cabela's: World's Foremost Outfitter: A History*, September 15, 2001.

[9] "The Customer Service Champs," *Business Week*, March 3, 2008, pg. 049.

[10] Vince Burks, "Customer Relations Begins With Employees," *O'Dwyer's Inside News of Public Relations & Marketing Communications*, March 17, 2012.

[11] Carl Sewell and Paul B. Brown, *Customers For Life*, Pocket Books, 1990.

[12] Nordstrom Company History, www.Nordstrom.com

[13] Ibid.

[14] Robert Spector and Patrick D. McCarthy, *The Nordstrom Way to Customer Service Excellence: The Handbook for Becoming the "Nordstrom of Your Industry,"* 2012, John Wiley & Sons.

[15] Wikipedia and www.xavier.edu/xlc/about/Customer-Service-A-Culture,-Not-a-Department.cfm.

[16] Robert Spector and Patrick D. McCarthy, *The Nordstrom Way to Customer Service Excellence: A Handbook For Implementing Great Service in Your Organization*, 2005, John Wiley & Sons.

[17] Robert Spector and Patrick D. McCarthy, *The Nordstrom Way to Customer Service Excellence: The Handbook for Becoming the "Nordstrom of Your Industry,"* 2012, John Wiley & Sons.

[18] Carl Sewell and Paul B. Brown, op.cit.

[19] E-mails with Deborah Gardner, April-May 2008, and www.competebetternow.com.

[20] Ibid.

[21] "The Customer-Centric Organization: From Pushing Products to Winning Customers," Booz Allen Hamilton, November 2003, www.boozallen.com.

[22] Amazon annual report, April 13, 2012, www.amazon.com/ir.

[23] Jeff Bezos, "Letter to Shareholders," Amazon annual report. op.cit.

[24] Ibid.

[25] Booz Allen Hamilton, op.cit.

[26] "Florida Ritz-Carlton Honors 'Whites-Only' Policy," www.bossip.com, April 24, 2012

[27] Ibid.

[28] Interview, emails with Paul Witting during February 2013.

[29] "Fidelity Honored As America's Winningest Brokerage Firm by Corporate Insight's 2011 E-Monitor Awards," www.fidelity.com/inside-fidelity/, March 6, 2012.

[30] Interview with Bradley D. Tilden, February 21, 2013.

[31] Ibid.

[32] John Gillie, "Alaska Airlines wins J.D. Power customer satisfaction award for fifth time," *The News Tribune*, Tacoma, Washington, June 13, 2012.

[33] Carl Sewell and Paul B. Brown, op.cit.

Chapter II

Listening

Listening is one of the essentials of good customer service. Listening is essential to communicating, negotiating, resolving conflicts and avoiding crises. Listening is hard work. For some people, it is very difficult, but it is a trait that can be learned. Listening is truly an admirable and enviable art for those who listen well.

From our earliest childhood development years, we all are taught how to speak, read and write. However, no one teaches us how to listen.

Several years ago, a student took a $10,000 bet that he could go through a year at college without speaking a word. He was well prepared with tape-recorded answers and flash cards so he could communicate. He said he wanted to be a good listener. It was not reported whether or not he won the bet.

Stephen R. Covey ranks listening as one of his seven habits of highly effective people. "Seek first to understand, then to be understood," he says. "Most people don't listen with the intent to understand; they listen with the intent to reply. They're either speaking or preparing to speak."[34]

"The ability to listen to others is essential," says Harvard University's Dr. Lawrence Susskind, conflict resolution guru and author of *Dealing With an Angry Public*. "When high-ranking spokespersons or executives are being assaulted by those who are fearful, anxious, and angry, they must put aside their own feelings and defensiveness so they can listen carefully and hear what people have to say.

"Good leaders must be as keyed into their audience's interests as their own," Susskind adds. "You will not be able to acknowledge the concerns of others if you cannot hear them. Listening must be active. This means reiterating what has been heard to be sure the message has been received."[35]

"In the digital marketplace, companies must improve social listening capabilities and apply predictive analytics designed to quickly identify and respond to potential customer issues before problems arise," says Robert Wollan, global managing director of Accenture Sales & Customer Service.[36]

Good Leaders Are Active Listeners

J. Willard "Bill" Marriott, Jr. believes that listening is the single most important on-the-job skill a good manager can cultivate. "A leader who doesn't listen well risks missing critical information, losing (or never winning) the confidence of staff and peers and forfeiting the opportunity to be a proactive, hands-on manager," he says. "Listening is how you empower people to grow in their jobs and gain confidence as decision makers. Listening is foremost an opportunity to learn."[37]

One successful executive who listens is Mark Cuban. He was a teenage entrepreneur. His first job was as a bartender. Then he founded dot.com and computer technology companies. He owns the Dallas Mavericks professional basketball team, a film and television production company, and a chain of movie theaters.

Cuban stays close with the team's fans and likes to keep them happy. While the cost of tickets to all National Basketball Association games has soared in recent years, he has always kept a number of Mavericks' tickets at a $2 price so any fan can afford to attend a game and bring a family.

He also posts his email address on the team's website so any fan or season ticket holder can email him. He personally reads and responds to each one whether it is from a fan, adversary or someone trying to sell him something.

Cuban and the team have supported the Dallas community. Because of a lack of funding, the city was faced with not having its annual St. Patrick's Day parade for the first time in 33 years. He stepped forward and wrote a check to the organizers to cover the cost. Maybe that's why he's also worth $2.8 billion.

Greg L. Michel, president of Crystal Cruise Lines, attributes the customer service success of his company to listening and anticipating. Crystal is consistently ranked #1 in its category for cruise ships.

In any conflict or negotiation you must be an active listener. Focus on the speaker and your adversaries, take notes, ask questions and make eye contact so they know you are listening. According to Covey, words represent only 10 percent of communication. The sounds we make and our inflection represent 30 percent and our body language 60 percent. [38]

Remember that the less you say, the more someone else will be able to remember what you say. It is just as important for someone listening to you to fully understand your message as it is for you to understand what they are saying. Saul Alinsky, who wrote the bible on nonviolent disruption, *Rules for Radicals*, says it best: "If you try to get your ideas across to others without paying attention to what they have to say, you can forget about the whole thing."[39]

Sam Walton's Rules

Entrepreneur and founder Sam Walton made customer service a priority at Walmart from the very beginning. In his book, *Made In America*, Walton, outlined 10 rules that worked for him in running a successful company. Two of his rules are specific to customer service – listening and to exceed your customers' expectations.[40]

"Listen to everyone in your company, and figure out ways to get them talking. The folks on the front lines – the ones who actually talk to the customer – are the only ones who really know what's going on out there," he wrote. "You'd better find out what they know. To push responsibility down in your organization, and to force good ideas to bubble up, you must listen to what your associates are trying to tell you."

Walton believed if you exceed your customers' expectations they will come back over and over. "Give them what they want – and a little more. Let them know you appreciate them" he wrote. His rules also included a commitment to your business so everyone will see and catch your passion; share profits with associates, treat them as partners and let them know you appreciate what they do; motivate partners and communicate everything with them; control expenses; ignore conventional wisdom and swim upstream; and celebrate successes.[41]

Walton died in 1992 and it is obvious that Walmart associates, or employees, are not treated or appreciated the way he outlined in his rules. For the past 10 years employees have been unhappy and protested about low wages, health insurance coverage, working conditions, and racial and gender discrimination. The employees have been joined by labor unions, community groups, grassroots organizations, religious organizations, environmental groups and even customers.[42]

Walmart has nearly 2.2 million employees worldwide and has faced a myriad of lawsuits and issues with regards to low wages, poor working conditions, inadequate health care and its strong anti-union policies. Approximately 70 percent of its employees leave within the first year.[43] Companies with outstanding customer service point to happy employees and a low turnover rate.

This wouldn't happen today if Walton were still alive. He had a special rapport with his employees and looked to them for feedback on customer service. According to legend, he often would buy a box of donuts on his way to the office and then stop at the loading dock. He would ask the employees to get coffee and join him while he handed out the donuts and asked them for their opinion. Some of the most successful CEOs still make a point of meeting with their lowest level employees.

Critics claim the company undercuts its competition with low prices because of government subsidies. A 2004 study by the University of California, Berkeley, said Walmart's low wages and benefits were insufficient and California taxpayers paid $86 million a year to the company's employees.[44]

With the expansion of Medicaid under Obamacare in 2013, the company stopped providing health insurance for employees who work fewer than 30 hours a week, shifting this burden to the federal government.[45]

Walmart has spent considerable time in court in the U.S. and foreign countries. In 2008 the Mexico Supreme Court of Justice ordered the company to cease paying its employees in part with vouchers redeemable only at Walmart stores.[46] This would be comparable to the company stores in Appalachia once owned by coal mine operators.

The company faced a class action lawsuit in Missouri in 2005 alleging that 160,000 to 200,000 were forced to work off-the-clock, denied overtime pay and were not allowed to take rest and lunch breaks.[47] In following years there was similar litigation in Pennsylvania, Oregon and Minnesota.

If he were alive today I wonder how Walton would respond to the numerous jokes and complaints that are regularly posted on social media and Internet blogs about Walmart.

Covey's Recommendations

You have to be an active listener to anticipate the actions of others. When you listen, you want to put yourself in their shoes and think like them. Understand their point of view. And, realize that acknowledging a point of view is not the same as agreeing with it. Covey points out several ways to acknowledge that you understand:

"As I get it, you believe ...

"So, as you see it ...

"You place a high value on ...

"What I guess I'm hearing is ...

"As I hear it, you ...

"You must have felt ..."

In his 7 Habits training, Covey points out there are five levels of listening, which he describes as follows:

"Ignoring: making no effort to listen.

"Pretend listening: make believe or give the appearance you are listening.

"Selective listening: hearing only what interests you.

"Attentive listening: paying more attention; being focused.

"Empathic listening: listening with eyes, heart and mind."

He says empathic listening, the highest level of listening, gets inside another person's frame of reference so you understand that person emotionally as well as intellectually. You give them emotional air to breathe.[48]

It is important for everyone in a company, organization and institution to practice and build listening skills.

Endnotes

[34] Stephen R. Covey, *7 Habits of Effective People,* Fireside, Simon & Schuster, Inc., 1990.

[35] Lawrence Susskind and Patrick Field, *Dealing With An Angry Public,* The Free Press, Simon & Schuster, Inc., 1996.

[36] "Consumers Defect in Growing Numbers But Majority Say 'You Could Have Kept Me,' Accenture Research Finds," December 5, 2012, www.accenture.com.

[37] J.W. Marriott, Jr. and Kathi Ann Brown, *Without Reservations – How A Family Root Beer Stand Grew Into A Global Hotel Company,* Luxury Custom Publishing, San Diego, 2013.

[38] Stephen R. Covey, op.cit.

[39] Saul D. Alinsky, *Rules For Radicals,* Vintage Books, a division of Random House, March 1972.

[40] Sam Walton with John Huey, *Made In America,* Doubleday, June 1992, Bantam Books, June 1993

[41] Ibid.

[42] Marcus Kabel, "Walmart, Critics Slam Each Other on Web," *The Washington Post*, July 18, 2006 and Jeff M. Sellers, "Deliver Us From Walmart," *Christianity Today*, July 31, 2006.

[43] "Store Wars When Walmart Comes to Town," *PBS*, February 24, 2007.

[44] Dube Arindrajit and Ken Jacobs, "Hidden Cost of Walmart Jobs," *University of California, Berkeley*, August 2, 2004.

[45] Alice Hines, "Walmart's New Health Care Policy Shifts Burden to Medicaid, Obamacare," *Huffington Post*, December 1, 2012; Napp Nazworth, "With Obamacare Walmart Shifts Employee Health Costs to Taxpayers," *Christian Post*, December 3, 2012.

[46] Joe Shaulis, "Mexico Supreme Court orders Walmart to stop paying workers in store vouchers," *Jurist*, September 5, 2008.

[47] "Walmart to face employee suit in Missouri," *USA Today*, November 2, 2005.

[48] Steven Covey, op.cit.

Chapter III

Responding

Early in my career I had a great boss and mentor who taught me to promptly return every telephone call and answer every letter. It was some of the best advice I've ever been given. Since then I added faxes to the list, and with new technology today, emails and text messages.

In addition to following this policy, I believe it is important to set a time limit for the response, such as 72 hours. I have established this as a policy for all employees reporting to me. Whenever possible, I recommend all phone calls, emails, texts and faxes be responded to within 24 hours. When someone is on travel or vacation, and technology permits, leave a voicemail message for the caller and an "out of office" response on email. If you are unable to respond, have a secretary or associate follow through.

As with any rule, there are exceptions – junk mail, spam and the robodialed telephone calls. Do not even attempt to ask to be removed from some spam emails because there could be a virus lurking once it is opened.

I've always responded to both job seekers and vendors with personal letters, not form letters. Unfortunately, too many senior managers today do not even bother to respond even with form letters to anyone. What I consider plain, old fashioned courtesy and just being polite does pay rewards. Years after giving job seekers some encouragement, one day I had a cold call from the public relations director of a major company. He said my letter gave him some words of encouragement that he never forgot and believed it help him get a job he wanted at the time. Because I followed a simple practice that I thought was good business, I was rewarded – he retained my firm for his company's business.

Ignoring a phone call, email, letter, text or fax can lead to an expensive, embarrassing and reputation damaging crisis. Examples will be cited in subsequent chapters.

The "Do Not Respond" Email

Nothing is more insulting to a consumer than to receive a "Do Not Respond" or "Do Not Reply" email when the issue is still open and you would like to respond. The sender is basically telling the recipient to just go away, don't bother us, don't call us, we'll call you. There are exceptions when there really is no need at all to reply or it is basically an information only message.

Running a close second to the "Do Not Reply" email is when the sender makes it difficult for the recipient to respond. Too many people who pretend to be in customer service and use such a title require the customer or client to click on a URL that will take them to the website location of the organization. Then one has to click on "contact" and follow instructions such as picking one of a few already pre-determined reasons or subjects for the email, often followed by a sub-subject, none of which may even be pertinent to the issue, and then a space to leave a message restricted by numbers of words.

There is no way the customer can reconnect with the individual who initially sent the one-way email because there is no way to list a name or title on most of the forms. In most cases there is no way for the customer to even keep a copy of the email by either listing his or her email address or printing out a hard copy.

The techies who created the system, obviously with the approval of management, and the "customer service" people using it, both need an explanation of what customer service is all about and a remedial course in customer service.

Communicators Need to Communicate

Professionals in the communications business often are the worst personal communicators. A good example is a former dean of the School of Journalism and Public Relations at University of Southern California. When Carol Burnett received a $1.6 million libel settlement from the *National Enquirer*, she asked our public relations agency what she should do with the money. The recommendation, made by one of my partners at ICPR, Los Angeles, was to give it to a university to teach ethics in journalism. He was a USC alumnus and Burnett asked him to arrange a meeting for her with the dean, but not to mention her name or details of the proposed gift.

Over a three-day period, my partner called the dean several times but could never speak with him. He was blocked each time by an overzealous gate guard who wanted to know more than he could tell her. The fact that he gave his name, phone number, and said he was a USC journalism school graduate should have been more than sufficient. The dean never returned his calls.

On the fourth day, when no meeting had been set and Burnett heard about the unreturned phone calls, she said she was not going to give money to someone responsible for teaching students how to communicate who couldn't communicate himself. She decided to give the money to Pepperdine University and asked our firm to release a story stating why. When it appeared on page one of *The Los Angeles Times* the university did everything it could to resolve the matter, but time had run out. The fallout was devastating to USC for a number of years. Because of the actions or inaction of the dean, gifts to the department dropped substantially.

Always Say "Thank You"

A philanthropist gave $20,000 to a chemistry professor at Texas A&M University but the professor was upset because he wanted $100,000. The benefactor also was planning to give a major gift in the $1 million plus range to another department at the university. After several weeks passed and the philanthropist had not received a "thank you" from the professor, he called to be sure his gift had gone through as planned and he hoped the professor was pleased.

The chemistry professor never had the courtesy to thank his benefactor, either verbally or in writing, and refused to return repeated telephone calls. Because the professor was tenured and under the umbrella of "academic freedom," his department head, dean, provost and president of the university did not intervene. The benefactor not only cut the chemistry department off from any future gifts, but cancelled his $1 million gift as well. At a conference of leaders in higher education, I cited this as an example to a panel of deans and provosts and asked how each would have handled the incident by demanding the professor issue an apology or issue a public reprimand to the professor. Not one panelist responded.

Take A Lesson From Southern Hospitality

Since the early days of the Colonies, The South has always been known for its hospitality. And Virginia is the epitome of Southern graciousness, politeness and hospitality. Any doubters need only to take a trip to Lexington, Virginia and visit the campus of Washington & Lee University. The university was founded in 1749 and named in honor of George Washington and Robert E. Lee. Thanks to a generous $20,000 endowment in 1796 by Washington the university survived. Lee became president in late 1865 and his innovative leadership took W&L into the national limelight. He established the law school and the university became the first college in the U.S. to offer programs in business and journalism.

Lee also established an informal code of conduct that led to W&L's Honor System. "We have but one rule here," he wrote, "and that is that every student be a gentleman."

A notable tradition at W&L is the "Speaking Tradition" where everyone speaks to everyone else. Visitors and guests walking across campus will be welcomed by anyone they meet – students, professors and members of the administration. The cadets from the

Virginia Military Institute, which abuts the W&L campus, follow this tradition when they cross the campus walking to downtown Lexington.

Two prominent graduates are proud that this tradition became an important part of their lives. "The speaking tradition is something I still adhere to. It is something I still do without thinking and it was part of being a Washington & Lee Gentleman," says Gary McPherson, who played basketball for the Generals from 1954-1958 in the last class to receive athletic scholarships. He was recruited with a football scholarship but the sport was dropped before his freshman year. After graduating, he returned to Lexington to be head basketball coach at VMI from 1963-1969. He is now senior director of development for the Mountaineer Athletic Club at West Virginia University.

For years W&L was all-male and had another tradition – a dress code that required a coat and tie at all times. For two years McPherson served on a committee responsible for disciplining any student who violated the code. The university no longer has a suit and tie dress code for men. Women were first admitted to W&L in 1985.[49]

Thornton M. "Tim" Henry, a prominent attorney in West Palm Beach, Florida, remembers when all freshman wore beanies until homecoming. "We were definitely easy to spot and were dressed down if we did not greet everyone," says Henry, who received his bachelor's degree in 1966 and law degree in 1969. "Once one gets into the habit of politely welcoming others, it does in fact carry over for the rest of your life. This is the hallmark of a Washington & Lee Gentleman."

Henry captained the soccer team his senior year, was All-Virginia for four years. For more than 30 years he held the W&L scoring record.[50]

Jeffrey G. Hanna, executive director of communications and public affairs for W&L, says that students today learn about the Speaking Tradition during their recruitment and once they are on campus are encouraged to continue it. "I won't try to tell you that every student looks up from his or her cell phone every time they greet someone on campus," Hanna adds, "But I do think the tradition remains very much alive here.

"Graduates tell of stories where they have become so used to the Speaking Tradition they are brought up short when they say "hello" to a stranger on a city street and do not get a response, or at least not the response to which they are accustomed." [51]

This author believes that the curse of modern technology is destroying tradition and common courtesy, customer service, and contributing to a rude society in which we live.

Hanna notes that the Speaking Tradition resulted in one of the university's most important gifts. "In the early 1900s, Mr. and Mrs. Robert Doremus stopped in Lexington on their way back to New York City after visiting the University of Virginia in Charlottesville. Once on campus, they were greeted by a student who put down his books and gave them a tour.

"Mr. Doremus, a wealthy stockbroker, was so impressed by the student's friendliness that he provided in his will that upon the death of Mrs. Doremus, their entire estate should be given to Washington & Lee.

"After Mr. Doremus's death in 1913, his widow gave the university a gift to build the Doremus Memorial Gymnasium and indoor swimming pool. W&L received the balance of the state upon her death in 1936," Hanna said.

Kenneth P. Ruscio told that story when he was inaugurated as W&L's president in 2006. "The couple had no prior connection to W&L but were given a clear impression of that it was a welcoming and friendly place. Originally the University of Virginia was to be the recipient of their largesse, but their minds were changed by the uncommon civility of this campus," Ruscio said. "Though the Doremus gift was the consequence of the Speaking Tradition and not its beginning, it serves as a tangible reminder why respect for others, whether friends or strangers, is a defining quality of our culture."

It proves that just being nice, polite and practicing common courtesy can pay millions in rewards.

Why Should I Buy Your Product or Service?

We have a generation of CEOs and senior managers today who cannot answer what should be the easiest question ever posed to them: Why should I buy your product of service? Unfortunately, most are unable to respond.

Corporate America, academia and nonprofits need leaders like Donald R. Keough. When he was president, chief operating officer and a director of Coca-Cola he always had an answer.

"If someone posed that question to me, my answer would simply be that I am surprised he or she did not have a chance to enjoy Coca-Cola in their lifetime because they have missed some very pleasant moments. Coca-Cola is simply a product to enjoy – to refresh you or when you need a chance to relax. These could be very pleasurable moments throughout your life," says Keough.

"Throughout the years all of our employees have a wide variety of jobs – but at the end of the day, they should asked themselves what is their basic responsibility. The best answer was given by a well-known general counsel of the company before my time. He was considered one of the brilliant lawyers in America. When asked his business, he replied: 'I sell Coca-Cola.'

"In fact, he was saying that he handled the legal aspects of the company to make certain that the Coca-Cola Company had the best possible highway to run on to sell its products throughout the world," Keough added.[52]

No Response = No Sale

Joan Short is president of WorldWide Golf & Travel, Inc., a travel agency in Newport Beach, California. Firms like hers are the life-blood of cruise lines and tour operators. Most of Short's clients want, and are willing to pay for exceptional service. They look to her for guidance, and not the Internet for the best discount price. She booked one of her clients in the penthouse suite on Celebrity Cruises' luxury Azamara Journey, a ship that has only 355 state-rooms.

When her client returned from what was described as a "cruise out of Hell," she wrote Celebrity's president, Daniel J. Hanrahan, detailing the problems and letting him know it was the first time in her 16 years in the business that something like this had happened.

Hanrahan did not respond personally to Short. The job was assigned to an "executive representative," a Beverly Boys-Brown, who eventually did contact her. Short asked that an apology be sent to her client. Then another "executive representative" sent a letter to her client with a $700 certificate for his next cruise on the Azamara. "It was not much of a letter, and my client has vowed never to again sail on the Azamara," said Short. "He asked that I mail the certificate back to the president which I did."

This author emailed "customer service" (only a generic email address was listed) at Celebrity Cruises and also Lynn Sierra-Caro in public relations at publicly-held Royal Caribbean International, which owns Celebrity, asking for the company's response to this case history. No one from either customer service or public relations responded, but Faye Miles, another "executive representative," sent an apologetic e-mail. Royal Caribbean makes it impossible to respond to any "executive representative." None have personal emails, which I find highly unusual for any "executive" so empowered and in authority. My only way to respond was to use a generic web cruise comments email that is always answered by another and different "executive representative." Neither do any of these "executives" have personal contact information such as a direct-dial phone number or even a mailing address.

The failure to communicate will cost Royal Caribbean, and all of its brands, untold revenues in the future from Short, and her clients, friends, and contacts in the travel business.

The Worst Communicators

People often ask me my opinion of who are the worst communicators. As group, I believe the management leaders in the following groups just never learned proper business etiquette and manners. I rank them as follows:

1. *Media* – Journalists are the most demanding when they want a response from someone for a quote or story, but very, very slow to respond, if at all, when even a fellow journalist is seeking information. In many cases forget it if you correct the journalist regarding an error.

Alan Hirsch, president of G+A Communications, New York, collects articles when the news media ignores requests for comments or just responds with a "no comment."[53] He has cited *The New York Times*, ABC network, Time Warner and others for having a double standard.

2. *Education* – There are problems at all levels and failure by many in higher education that have cost their institutions millions. This goes back to people who train the future administrators, professors, deans, provosts, presidents and teachers. One of the worst incidents in my recent experience was with the dean of a school of education.

3. *Entertainment, Television and Motion Pictures* – The worst offenders in this group are the young publicity flacks who are too impressed with their own importance and become overzealous gate guardians. The old guard agents and public relations representatives are no problem at all and always respond.

4. *Public Relations Practitioners* – People in this group are supposed to be professional communicators when in fact, many are not even professional. Again, much of the problem lies with young people in the profession. The best in the business are also the best at always responding. Many do not have the proper training or mentoring.

5. *Tecchies* – Whenever I need to contact anyone in this field, and especially in Silicone Valley, I feel an air of arrogance. The problem starts with the CEO and I have found that is rampant throughout the companies. That could have been a reason for the first dot.com bust

and why the price of publicly-held stocks take a nose dive after an initial public offering.

Endnotes

[49] Emails and conversations with Gary McPherson, January-February 2013.

[50] Emails with Thornton M. Henry, Esq., January-February 2013.

[51] Emails with Jeffrey G. Hanna, November-December 2012 and January 2013.

[52] Letter of March 24, 2013 from Donald R. Keough.

Chapter IV

Telephone Etiquette

A voice on the telephone is often the first impression a future customer, potential client, stakeholder, or investor has of a company or organization. The people who answer the telephone are responsible for the image the company projects to the public. Are they polite? Pleasant? Responsive?

No company wants the reputation of being arrogant, rude or uncaring, yet many do because of the way employees handle telephone calls. But how many CEOs ever assess the way calls are handled in their business? Some organizations even block public access by not listing telephone, fax or e-mail addresses on the letterhead of some senior executives. This practice only exacerbates problems and speaks volumes about the company's customer service attitude.

Do you answer your calls? Or do you delegate this to a secretary? When they are not in meetings and available in their offices, communicative executives answer their own telephones. This immediately assures the caller of access and reinforces the executive's concern for business.

The obvious screen, "Who's calling please?" always sounds a bit phony, especially when the screener puts the caller on hold, and then comes back on the line and says: "I'm sorry, Mr. So-and-So isn't in right now." This always leaves the thought in the back of my mind, "Is he really out, or is he just ducking me?"

John B. DeFrancesco, co-founder of DeFrancesco-Goodfriend Associates, Chicago, which is now a part of L. C. Williams & Associates, believes business telephone etiquette is an important and often overlooked public relations tool. He asks: "Are your employees guilty of ignoring courteous telephone procedure? If so, you could be losing valuable business. Most executives know the importance of making a good first impression. Poor telephone manners can result in prospects or disgruntled customers going somewhere else when they are treated rudely on the phone."

In a poll conducted by his firm, 40 percent of business executives are either "usually dissatisfied" or "sometimes dissatisfied" with the way their calls are handled by a receptionist or secretary. Less than half were "usually satisfied" and only 16 percent "sometimes satisfied." DeFrancesco cites the following as a short list of major offenses cited by survey participants:

- Being placed on hold too long was by far the most exasperating phone discourtesy, noted by 76 percent.
- Unreturned phone calls, 59 percent.
- Screening of calls, 36 percent.
- General lack of courtesy, 22 percent.
- Asking "who is calling," 22 percent.
- Background music while on hold, 18 percent.

According to Advantage Media, Inc. of Chatsworth, California, telephone courtesy does make a difference. "When callers are treated courteously, they normally respond by treating you more pleasantly and with greater respect," says Advantage Media. "Courtesy even helps irate or angry callers become more reasonable. ... Telephone courtesy not only smoothes your relationship with callers, it also helps you become the best you can be as a professional member of your organization's team."[53]

Modern technology has virtually destroyed the personal touch of customer service. The average American business executive spends some 60 hours a year on hold according to a survey by Accoun-temps. Many companies have caller ID and sophisticated software that lets them know in nanoseconds whether they are talking with Bill Gates or a store clerk. "For me, the most frustrating thing is that you can never get a person if you have some question you want to ask," says Dale Myers, a Philadelphia advertising saleswoman.[54]

Good telephone etiquette can be taken right to the bottom line. Dr. Robert Walker, vice president of development-emeritus for Texas A&M University, never allowed any of his calls to be screened and he promptly returns all calls. He also is a good listener and was well-rewarded one day by a woman who asked him a number of questions during a 30-minute conversation. At the end, the woman asked Walker to call her attorney to make arrangements for a $15 million gift she wanted to give the university. Just like the Doremus gift to Washington & Lee, her first choice was another university. However, on her first call, she could not get past the gate guard to speak with anyone in authority. Even though she had no direct con-tacts or past experience with Texas A&M, after hanging up from her first choice, she called the Aggie development office. One uni-versity's lack of respect for callers led to a generous gift for one who did understand the benefits of telephone etiquette.

Here are tips for good telephone etiquette:
- Good customer service may avoid creating an adversary or crisis and could even be considered for some, job insurance.
- Return all phone calls promptly.
- For whatever reason, if a call cannot be returned, have a col-league or associate respond.
- For voice mail, your greeting should include your name, the day and whether or not you are in town that day. If you plan to be out of town, let the caller know when you will return or refer to an associate with an extension number. The very best change their voice messages daily and at a minimum once a week.

- Never have another person place a call for you. Successful executives place their own telephone calls.
- Be sure all employees understand the organization's policy.
- Don't screen any phone calls. The only possible exception might be the most senior executives. State, local and federal government employees should take all calls without question.
- Always be courteous and say "please" and "thank you."
- If you're calling someone, give the secretary or receptionist your name. If you're not known to the individual you're calling, also give your title and the name of your organization.
- Identify yourself by name when you answer the phone. In large organizations it's also a good idea to also identify your department.
- If it is late in the day, and calls can't be returned because you are in a meeting, have an associate or secretary return the call, and let the caller know when you will be able to return the call. If the call is important, give the caller your home number or ask the caller for his or her home number.
- It is important to let the caller know when you can return a call. An extended meeting may prevent a call from being returned one day, but let the caller know if you will be in meetings the next day or even going out of town.
- News media representatives work on tight deadlines. All media calls should be returned promptly, or immediately referred to the public relations office for response.
- Keep a log of all incoming and outgoing phone calls with day, date, and time. Then you know exactly when someone called you or when you called someone else. Go an additional step and note the subject of the call.
- Take accurate and complete messages with the name of the caller, company, time, date the message was received, action to be taken, and the name of the person taking the message.

- If you are not certain how a name is spelled, politely ask the caller to spell it for you.
- When leaving a message, give your name slowly, repeat it and spell out. Slowly give and repeat your telephone number.
- Do not call people before 9 a.m. and after 9 p.m. unless it is an emergency or you have been asked to do so.
- Be aware of the four time zones in the U.S. China is one country that does not have time zones.

Endnotes

[53] *Jack O'Dwyer's Newsletter*, January 1, 1997, pg. 3.

[54] William Bunch, "Call it customer disservice," *Philadelphia Daily News*, Philadelphia, Pennsylvania, August 8, 2001.

Chapter V

More Strategies & Practices

When you think of customer service you don't expect to get advice from a Hall of Fame football coach. However, one person who has excellent advice is Lou Holtz, a retired coach, author, television analyst and a motivational speaker. Here is what he says about "what our customers mean to us."[55]

- Customers are the most important people in our business.
- Customers do not depend on us, we depend on them.
- Customers never interrupt our work, they are our work.
- Customers do us a favor when they call; we don't do them favors by letting them in.
- Customers are part of our business, not outsiders.
- Customers are flesh-and-blood human beings, not cold statistics.
- Customers bring us their wants; we fulfill them.
- Customers are not to be argued with.
- Customers deserve courteous attention.
- Customers are the lifeblood of this, and every other business.
- Customers are who we are when we're not working (So let's treat them the way we want to be treated ourselves!).

Poor Customer Service Affects Profits

Just as good customer service will build a business, and often allow a company to charge more for its products and services than the competition, bad customer service affects profits. Several years ago, McDonald's learned that rude employees cost the company an average of $60,000 in lost sales at each restaurant. This amounted to an annual corporate loss of $750 million.[56]

In the comic strip Shoe, the creator had one character saying, "My boss said that I'm rude, have a bad attitude, and lousy people skills." The response was, "So that's how you got promoted to customer service!"[57]

Michael Bloomberg, Mayor of New York City, fired the head of the customer service office for an essay he posted on the Internet. Fletcher Vredenburgh said he was responsible for handling complaints from "griping, often whining, often stupid New Yorkers."[58]

Some 80 percent of adults polled in a 2007 Harris Interactive poll vowed never to buy from the same company after a negative experience, up from 68 percent in 2006. Pushed to the point of frustration with customer representatives both online and by phone, 28 percent said they cursed and 19 percent admitted to shouting. The poll showed regional differences, with 83 percent of Westerners saying they will never do business again with the offending company. Southerners are least likely to swear, but 12 percent fantasized about picketing or defacing the company's headquarters. The biggest swearers were 34 percent of the people in the Midwest. In the Northeast, the respondents were unlikely to get emotional, file a complaint, or give a bad review, but just take their business elsewhere.[59]

An earlier poll of 2,013 adults by Public Agenda, a New York based nonprofit organization, said a lack of respect and courtesy in the U.S. is a serious problem, and 61 percent said it only keeps getting worse. The organization reported that poor customer service had become so rampant that it caused nearly 50 percent of those surveyed to walk out of a store.[60]

Modern technology has made it easy for the consumer to be heard. Angry consumers who can't get satisfaction from a company now post their complaints on blogs or websites such as The Consumerist (www.consumerist.com) where they can share their problem with hundreds of thousands, or even millions of potential customers. Some have videotaped their problems to post on You Tube (www.youtube.com).

In its cover story on customer service, *Business Week* magazine wrote that 2007 will be the year fed-up consumers finally dropped the hammer. In a story titled "Consumer Vigilantes," the subhead was most appropriate: "Memo to Corporate America: Hell now hath no fury like a customer scorned." The magazine cited numerous case histories of how consumers fought back from actual near violence to get attention in an office, to posting on the web shortcut telephone numbers to quickly reach a live person at a call center.[61]

Dr. Leonard L. Berry, one of the gurus of customer service, is a professor of marketing at Texas A&M University and the author of two books – *On Great Service* and *Discovering the Soul of Service*. He lists the following as the top 10 customer service complaints:[62]

1. *True Lies*. Blatant dishonesty including selling unneeded services or quoting fake, low estimates.

2. *Red Alert*. Companies that assume customers are stupid and treat them accordingly.

3. *Broken Promises*. Service providers who do not show up on time or provide poor service.

4. *I Just Work Here*. Employees who are not empowered to resolve the problem.

5. *The Big Wait*. A line made long because too few checkout lanes are open.

6. *Automatic Pilot*. Impersonal, going-through-the-motions non-service.

7. *Suffering In Silence*. Employees who don't bother to tell customers how a problem will be resolved.

8. *Don't Ask*. Employees who seem put out by requests for help.

9. *Lights On, No One Home*. Clueless employees who can't answer simple questions.

10. *Misplaced Priorities*. Workers who conduct personal business while the customer waits.

Customers For Life

Carl Sewell's philosophy is to turn a one-time buyer into a lifetime customer. He built Sewell Automotive Companies, Dallas, Texas, into the leading luxury automobile dealer in the U.S., growing from $10 million in sales in 1968 to more than $250 million just 20 years later. Today the company sells Cadillac, Lexus, Audi, Infinity, Buick, GMS, MINI, Subaru and Masaerati cars in Dallas, Forth Worth, Grapevine, Houston, Plano, and San Antonio, Texas.

The business was started in 1911 by his father, Carl Sewell, Sr., as a car dealership, hardware store and movie theater. The Sewell philosophy that continues today was that it is not important what is being sold, but how the customer is treated.

When the Great Depression hit in 1929 the three banks closed where the company had all its money deposited. So, the senior Sewell relocated to the tiny town of Crane in the West Texas oilfields and started over. In 1941 he moved the business back to Dallas, survived World War II, and built a loyal following as a Lincoln-Mercury-Ford dealership in the 1940s and 1950s.

Sewell has 10 commandments of customer service:

1. *Bring 'em back alive*. Ask customers what they want and give it to them again and again.

2. *Systems, not smiles.* Saying please and thank you doesn't insure you'll do the job right the first time, every time. Only systems guarantee you that.

3. *Underpromise, overdeliver.* Customers expect you to keep your word. Exceed it.

4. *When the customer asks, the answer is always yes.* Period.

5. *Fire your inspectors and consumer relations department.* Every employee who deals with clients must have the authority to handle complaints.

6. *No complaints? Something's wrong.* Encourage customers to tell you what you're doing wrong.

7. *Measure everything.* Baseball teams do it. Football teams do it. Basketball teams do it. You should, too.

8. *Salaries are unfair.* Pay people like partners.

9. *Your mother was right.* Show people respect. Be polite. It works.

10. *Japanese them.* Learn how the best really do it; make their systems your own. Then improve them.

He continues with a warning: "These ten rules aren't worth a damn … unless you make a profit. You have to make money to stay in business and provide good service.[63]

Sewell was the first auto dealer in Texas to provide free loan cars for service customers and to be open all day Saturday for service. The competition quickly followed his lead. He will deliver cars to people's homes on special occasions even if on a Sunday or holiday. All of his sales people and service advisers give customers their home telephone numbers and someone is at the dealership who can be called 24/7.

"We want people to call us, no matter what time it is," he says. "They're our customers and we want to take care of them. Besides, we would rather do the work than have our customers give it to somebody who might charge more and care less." His people respond to every need including a flat tire or if someone is locked out of their car.

He also has some great advice that is adaptable to any business, organization or institution:

"Good is never enough.

"Being first is not good enough.

"If an idea works in one place, you can be pretty certain it will work in another.

"There's no such thing as after hours.

"Make it easy for customers to complain.

"Let the customers help you provide good service.

"If you smile, odds are they'll smile back.

"The boss must set the example.

"You can't give good service if you sell a lousy product.

"Borrow from the best. Actively search for ideas to borrow."[64]

A Contrarian Philosophy

Jim Ukrop, along with his brother, grew a grocery business into a major regional supermarket chain of 29 stores and a specialty market by being different from his competition and investing in his employees.

His parents opened the first 500 square foot store in 1937 in a blue collar area of Richmond, Virginia and delivered groceries and provided credit to the customers, most of whom worked in the tobacco plants. He soon realized that while he was a good merchant and delivered quality service he was not very good at collecting credit. He changed his model by switching to a cash-and-carry operation. His new marketing plan was to forgive his customers' credit obligations and promise to lower prices. It worked. By the time he left to serve in World War II, his 3,000 square foot store was flourishing.

"We lived right next to the store and I started working at an early age moving boxes and putting up eggs. By the time I was 14, I was earning 50 cents an hour," Ukrop says. "For me, college was a four-year holiday!"

After graduating from The College of William & Mary in 1960, he turned down an offer to work for Kroger to stay in the family business. His first assignment was to train the bag boys and organize displays. By 1963, he had convinced his father to allow him to open a second store, which he managed. In 1965, the third store was opened and he became the company's general manager. By 1971, the original location was closed and the operation had added five additional stores when Jim's younger brother Bobby joined the operation; and together they worked to build the company.

"During the early years, I continued my Dad's philosophy of not wanting to see how big we could be, but how we could be better than anyone else," he added. "If you did the same things your competition did, how could you differentiate? During the 1960s many grocers were like horses going off a cliff following the others, but not knowing where they were going. They were chasing fads not trends."

With a policy of slow, but controlled growth, by 2010, when it sold to Ahold, a Dutch company, Ukrop's Super Markets had become a dominant regional chain.

"The grocery business has high capital and labor costs and low margins. It is a business of pennies and you have to be careful how you spend your money," Ukrop says. "Traditionally grocery chains spent 2 percent of sales on marketing and advertising. We believed the best way we could advertise was to create the best possible experience for our customers who would then let others know by word-of-mouth. We decided to spend only one-half of one percent on marketing and advertising. We didn't want to tell people how good we were, we wanted to show them. And our reputation spread.

"We used the other 1½ percent to invest in people – for more employees to better serve the customers in our markets, for training programs, and to pay them higher wages and benefits. The way you treat your employees is the way they will treat your customers. We never opened a new store until we knew we had the right people in place who could run the new supermarket as well as those we had already opened."

Ukrop's also was innovative. Their markets were the first in the area to make and sell prepared foods with no added preservatives. Along with Vons Supermarkets in California, Ukrop's was the first supermarket chain in the U.S. to create a frequent shopper card. He and his brother travelled throughout the U.S. and Europe to see what other industry leaders were doing that might be successful in the Richmond market. Soon management of grocery chains worldwide started visiting Ukrop's for ideas. "I remember one time in a store we had two groups of foreign visitors speaking different languages."

He also treated the customer as always being right even when the customer was wrong. When someone complained about being shortchanged, we took his or her word for it. Once a woman returned a bag of potato chips saying she bought more than she needed for a birthday party. Her money was "refunded" even though Ukrop's did not carry that brand. Half way through the store, she returned to the front and said, "I just remembered you are closed on Sundays and I purchased them elsewhere."

Before the days of credit cards, customers paid by cash or check. "Sometimes a customer might be short on cash or have forgotten the check book," he says. "We just asked them to sign a receipt and pay the next time they shopped.

"After checking out, if a customer discovered having a flat tire, we'd change the tire. If a customer lost car keys or was locked out of the car, we would drive the customer home."

Ukrop loves to tell the story of seeing an elderly woman in the produce department holding up a pineapple. "I asked her if she wanted only half and her eyes lit up when she said 'Yes, please.' When I returned with a half for her she said to me, 'I live alone and when I feel low I get in my car and drive to the nearest Ukrop's store because I always feel better when I come out of your store than when I entered.' Over the years other customers told similar stories."

When many supermarkets began having banks as part of their stores, Ukrop's resisted. However, in 1997 Ukrop's founded First

Market Bank, separate from the markets, and successfully applied the same management and customer service principles to its business.

"We created an environment at the bank where our people looked forward to coming to work, energized to work hard but have fun. We wanted an open culture. This philosophy has to start at the very top and work down, not in the middle of an organization. The people who came most in contact with our customers were generally the lowest paid.

"At the bank, our sales and support staff were all on one floor. The president was at one end of the bank and the CEO at the other. When they wanted to talk to each other, they passed by and interacted with all of the employees." First Market Bank was another success for the Ukrops and in 2010 they merged First Market with a larger bank.[65]

Satisfaction Guaranteed

In October 1989 Hampton Hotels offered the hospitality industry's first 100 percent satisfaction guarantee that states if for any reason guests are not completely satisfied with their stay, they will not be expected to pay. On their first day, employees must complete training on the 100 percent satisfaction guarantee and sign a training completion certificate. All Hampton Inns must participate in the program.

Hampton says its research shows that hotel employees take much more pride in their hotel and in their work, knowing that their hotel stands behind its product and service, and guarantees complete satisfaction to every guest. The hotel trains its employees to care about good service and teaches them the five secrets of customer loyalty:[66]

- I'll take care of that for you.
- Take responsibility.
- We want your business.
- Thank you for thinking of us. Thank you for your business.
- Consider it done.

Some years ago I stayed at a Hampton Inn in Wheeling, West Virginia and was awakened early by a wake-up call I did not request. After having the hotel's complimentary breakfast, I went to check out and was told there was no charge. I was satisfied with my stay and insisted on paying something, but the desk clerk said absolutely not. "Our goal is to provide the best accommodations and service in the lodging industry today," said Edward T. Hitchman III, the general manager. Why doesn't the entire hospitality industry adopt this guarantee?

Cabela's also has a 100 percent satisfaction guarantee. One loyal customer who has spent more than $12,000 over 20 years, returned a pair of hunting boots he bought four years earlier. There was no tread on the soles, and it was obvious the boots had been worn many times during the four years. The customer complained they just didn't fit right, and Cabela's gave him the benefit of the doubt that his boots just did not feel right for four years, so he was given his choice of a replacement pair or refund.[67]

"The two most important words I ever wrote were on that first Walmart sign: Satisfaction Guaranteed," according to Sam Walton. "Make good on all your mistakes, and don't make excuses – apologize. Stand behind everything you do."[68]

Avery Comarow, writes in *U.S. News & World Report* about his father going to Sears with a 30-year-old Craftsman mechanical screwdriver. In keeping with the company's no-questions-asked pledge since 1929 to replace any unsatisfactory Craftsman hand tool, he was given a new screwdriver. A number of companies provide customers with lifetime guarantees of their products. L. L. Bean, a company that consistently ranks very high on customer service lists, will provide a replacement, refund, or a charge credit. Le Creuset guarantees its cookware for 101 years. Briggs & Riley will replace a piece of luggage with a reconditioned one if it cannot be fixed.[69]

Be Wary of Rogue Employees

Consider what happened to one of the country's major homebuilders when a secretary didn't get back to a new home buyer, and even worse, make her boss aware of the situation. The customer's dishwasher wasn't working properly and she was hosting a dinner party on Saturday. She stayed home all day Thursday, waiting for a repairman who never arrived, and in spite of repeated calls to the builder on Friday, the same thing happened again. She had a multitude of errands to run Saturday.

The secretary considered the woman a chronic complainer, and just didn't like her. When the home owner called at 4:45 Friday afternoon, the secretary ignored her, and went home. During the dinner party, the conversation of he guests got around to how the builder was handling repairs, and how badly the host had been treated. Before the evening was over, all of the guests, who were new home buyers in the development, discussed problems with their houses that needed fixing. One of the dinner guests was an attorney who suggested a class-action law suit. The next day the entire new home community was mobilized, and by the time the secretary's boss got to work on Monday morning, a class-action suit had been filed asking for sales rescissions.

Not only did the home builder have to correct many more items than otherwise may have been needed, but a cash settlement and costly attorney's fees impacted quarterly earnings, tarnished its good reputation because of negative media exposure, and sparked action for class-action suits by homeowners in other subdivisions. What makes this crisis even worse is the fact that the homebuilder was one of the first to establish a customer relations department, and was well respected by its customers and fellow builders. However, when employees don't follow company policy, even the best programs can fail.

Pros and Cons of Outsourcing

"Sending jobs overseas may be good for the bottom line in the short term, but frustrated customers will vote with their wallets," says Dr. Bruce Weinstein, a professional ethicist.

"More and more businesses are outsourcing not just manufacturing jobs but service ones too. On the face of it, this seems like a smart financial move: By slashing labor costs 25 percent, 50 percent, or more, companies that have had slim profit margins are now able to enrich the bottom line and keep shareholders happy.

"Outsourcing customer service, however, is not only unethical. It's bad for business," Weinstein says. "The problem with outsourcing customer service is that this practice creates nothing but negative word of mouth."[70]

L.L. Bean, a 100-year-old, privately held, family-owned business in Freeport, Maine was ranked first in customer service in the fourth annual customer service awards by *Bloomberg Businessweek*. The retailer is known for its lenient returns policy, quality apparel and reliable outdoor equipment, and fast responses from its call centers. In 2009 it closed a call center and gave employees the option to work as home-based agents rather than outsourcing the work. "With outsourcing, you're just giving too much away," says Terry Sutton, vice president of customer satisfaction.[71]

Some years ago when I lived in a city where Neiman Marcus did not have a retail store I purchased two gifts through its catalog department. Neiman Marcus completely bungled both purchases. When I called to complain to a senior executive, I was told that this part of the business had been outsourced and that was why there was a problem. She told me that outsourcing had created a number of problems for the company and this policy was going to be reviewed. I haven't done business with them since.

An online website named eHow has more than one million articles and 170,000 videos and offers both pro and con views of outsourcing customer service.

Clernie Nye believes outsourcing keeps cost to a minimum, increases productivity, provides a competitive advantage, and businesses can focus on core areas. "Outsourcing call centers to India, which is many hours ahead of the U.S., means employees can work round the clock in order to serve customers in the U.S.," she writes. "This means keeping a 24-hour operation in place."[72]

Another eHow contributor, Luke Arthur, disagrees. "While outsourcing customer service could help the bottom line initially, it has some disadvantages that can affect the company in the future," he writes. "Outsourced customer service representatives lack the appropriate knowledge-base to adequately help customers since they do not work directly for the company. This is particularly true for technical issues.

"In many cases the representatives speak English as a second language which leads to frustration with the customers who often end up shopping elsewhere.

"Many Americans are loyal to companies that do not ship jobs overseas," he adds. "When they phone a call center and hear someone from another country, they may no longer wish to work with that company."

Unlike Nye, Arthur sees no competitive advantage. "Outsourcing leaves a major part of your business outside of your control."[73]

Customer service representatives must be able to communicate clearly according to Weinstein. "This also means that these employees should be fluent not only in the primary language of the customer base but in their culture, customers and idiosyncrasies as well."[74]

Too Many Complaints? Fire the Customers!

During the summer of 2007, and at the same time that Sprint Nextel Corp. launched an advertising campaign to attract new customers, the company disconnected more than 1,000 customers for complaining too much. "These customers were calling customer service lines to a degree that we felt was excessive," says Roni Singleton, public relations manager of corporate communications. "In some cases they were calling hundreds of times a month for a period of six to 12 months on the same issues even after we felt those issues had been resolved.

In December, the company named Daniel R. Hesse as CEO and he believed customer service was going to be one of his biggest challenges. In his very first operations meeting with senior management he saw that this subject was not even on the agenda. It now is the first issue discussed. Since merging in 2005, Sprint Nextel has ranked last among the country's five major wireless carriers in annual customer service surveys by J.D. Power & Associates.[75]

Service Is Critical Key to Restaurants

"In the past decade customer service in the restaurant business unfortunately became secondary to the egos of so many chefs who acquired international celebrity. Now, because of a challenging economy with fewer expense account customers and changes of customer dining patterns, that is turning around," says Sharon Van Vechten, renowned hospitality and fashion industry public relations and marketing consultant. "Restaurants are reversing their strategy and returning to some semblance of sanity by altering their 40- and 50-course tasting menus. Higher customer service undoubtedly will follow."

The headline in a *Vanity Fair* article by Corby Kummer, a prominent food writer, tells it all: "Tyranny – It's What's For Dinner. The reservation was nearly impossible to get. The meal will cost several hundred dollars. The chef is a culinary genius. But in the era of the four-hour, 40-course tasting menu, one key ingredient is missing: any interest in what (or how much) the customer wants to eat."[76]

Kummer writes that Charlie Trotter "helped unleash a generation of chefs no longer willing to take orders. The entire experience … display[s] the virtuosity not of cooks but of culinary artists. A diner's pleasure is secondary."[77] Van Vechten says that Trotter's restaurant in Chicago is one of the worlds finest and is known as being innovative and progressive in the world of food and wine and establishing new standards for fine dining worldwide.

Kummer's says Thomas Keller, chef and owner of The French Laundry in Yountville, California and Ferran Adrià of elBulli in Roses, Catalonia, Spain, "demand unconditional surrender from their customers." At one dining, Adrià served the customer 50 courses, and Keller 40 or more, and the customer didn't have a choice.[78] It was an eat and like it or else or take it or leave it scenario.

Called the most imaginative generator of haute cuisine on the planet, elBulli closed on July 30, 2011. Although the average cost of a meal was US$325, the small restaurant lost money for more than 10 years. It could only accommodate 8,000 diners a season but had more than two million requests. Five times it was rated #1 on the list of the world's top 50 restaurants by *Restaurant Magazine*. There is speculation it may reopen in 2014.[79] After his successful 25-year run as one of America's leading chefs, Charlie Trotter closed in August 2012.

Chef Grant Achatz's Alinea, in Chicago, was named the best restaurant in the U.S. by *Gourmet* a year after it opened. Achatz worked at elBulli. To dine at his second restaurant, Next, you make reservations like buying theater tickets and pay up to $300 when you book, and then use it or lose it. In minutes all tickets sold out for an entire year so seats to dine at Aliena are now on the same system.[80]

All celebrity chefs stress the importance of service and believe it is an equal half to the food on the plates. "Service is extremely important. People will come to the restaurant for food, but they'll come back for service," says Tom Colicchio owner of Craft and Colicchio and Sons restaurants in New York City and Las Vegas. "I'm a cook, first and foremost, and service is more important than food," according to Charlie Trotter. "Service can make or break a restaurant," says Tom Keller. "I think service is number one priority for us."[81]

"When Danny Meyer opened his first restaurant, Union Square Café in 1985 in New York City, he focused on customer satisfaction to make it successful," says Van Vechten, who was former director of public relations for Revlon, Inc. and a partner in a leading Hollywood entertainment company. Her hospitality marketing career covers three decades of wine and food promotions, multiple award-winning Relais & Chateaux resorts and five-star restaurants and branding New York's world famous Rainbow Room at Rockefeller Center, at one time the highest grossing and most photographed restaurant in the world. Meyer's restaurant has held the #1 spot nine times in the New York Zagat Survey of "Most Popular" restaurants. What is interesting is that both Trotter and Meyer got into cooking after graduating with degrees in political science – Trotter from the University of Wisconsin and Meyer from Trinity College.

Parisian Chef Alain Passard, in an interview with the *Financial Times*, when replying to a question about whether the customer is always right, said "Yes, always." The much honored Passard went on to add, "I am there to serve others' commands, and I always do what I am asked to do. I put aside my own concerned when faced with a client who orders a dish cooked a certain way or asks for a certain seasoning."[82]

"At the end of the day, when it comes to customer service, I believe people still want some luxury in their lives but are no longer willing or able to pay through the nose for it," Van Vechten adds. "With today's much savvier customer, customer service is more about five-star 'experiences' than just five-star places."

Geeks or Greeks?

Best Buy's Geek Squad at the Northgate Mall in Seattle practices customer service the way the Greeks have practiced fiscal responsibility. According to my good friend Richard, customer service was non-existent when he recently had a problem with his computer.

He called to explain his problem and was asked to bring his computer to the store. Here is what happened when he arrived at the store and went to the Geek Squad help desk.

GEEK #1 (while serving another customer) – Are you recycling that computer?

RICHARD – No.

GEEK #1 (in a demanding voice) – Put the computer over there! (He then went to another employee, ignoring Richard, and said "I'm going to lunch.")

After eight minutes passed, another Geek asked Richard if he had been helped. He replied "No" and explained what he needed. The Geek disappeared in a back room and then said someone would help in a minute.

Another eight minutes passed and a Geek named Tyler asked Richard to explain the problem.

RICHARD – The computer had a message that said to put in a new file and do a complete system root test. Everything passed.

GEEK TYLER – You need a new computer.

RICHARD – Does this mean that you will not try to put this file in and see if it works?

GEEK TYLER – No. You need a new computer.

RICHARD – What about saving my files?

GEEK TYLER – That will cost you $100 to get the files out and $70 for a backup hard drive. We sell Dell computers. Do you want to look at any?

RICHARD – But what about first looking at my computer?

GEEK TYLER – No.

RICHARD – When I called and talked to a woman she said to bring in my computer and someone would determine what, if anything is wrong.

GEEK TYLER – Your computer is broken. You need to buy a new one.

At this point Richard looked at several computers and chose one to buy, a Dell model 660.

RICHARD – Will my printer work with this?

GEEK TYLER – How old is your printer?

RICHARD – A little over five years old.

GEEK TYLER – Then you need a new printer. Do you have the disk for Word?

RICHARD – No I don't.

GEEK TYLER – Then you need to buy new Word because without it you will not be able to open your files.

The Geek left and turned Richard over to a sales lady.

FEMALE GEEK #1 – We don't have that Dell model in stock here. You have to go to another store (a 30-minutes drive away) where they have six in stock.

RICHARD – Does this mean I have to spend even more time now to go the other store, buy the new computer, and then bring it back here to get my files downloaded?

FEMALE GEEK #1 – Yes.

RICHARD – But can you cut me a deal if I do all of this work?

FEMALE GEEK #1 – (no response)

Richard then discussed the situation with the manager, Michael, who gave him a 10 percent discount. After going to the other store to pickup his new computer, Richard returned to encounter another female Geek.

FEMALE GEEK #2 – We will download your files into a backup hard drive.

RICHARD – Can I speak with Tyler?

FEMALE GEEK #2 (after going to the back room again) – He's too busy to speak to you.

Richard left and two days later called the Geek Squad. He was told they could not download the files, they would have to send it elsewhere, and the cost could be as much as $2,000. At this point he took both computers home and called his nephew who is a computer technician.

When the nephew arrived he downloaded the files in an hour and said the new computer came with Word so Richard did not need to buy the software and that a $5 flash drive would have accomplished what was needed rather than a $70 hard drive. Also, the old printer worked just fine with the new computer.

Richard returned to the store to buy the flash drive and get a refund for the "repair" of his old computer. When he explained his story to the manager, he apologized. But this same manager should be monitoring the employees he supervises.

All is well and Richard compliments Dell for its great customer service and says that technicians have called him a couple of times a week helping him learn how best to use the new computer. A plus for Dell, a minus for the Geeks who lost a customer for Best Buy.

Shawn Score, Best Buy's senior vice president of U.S. Retail, knows the company has "let its customer-service muscle atrophy." Score, who began selling camcorders and VCRs 26 years ago at a predecessor company, has identified and plans to fix problems that have led customers to walk out of stores without making a purchase.

These include apathetic sales clerks and several years of 60 percent employee turnover. He has increased sales training and rewards employees with pay incentives who increase sales and help their stores raise customer satisfaction scores.[83]

Gary Balter of Credit Suisse is one financial analyst who believes the company must repair its reputation for lack-luster service if it is to prosper. "People have started referring to the chain as 'that blue and gold store where the salesperson usually can't help you,'" he says.[84]

Get Customer Feedback

Smart, customer-service-oriented companies today ask their customers to let them know whether or not they are doing a good job. More executives could follow the lead of Mark Cuban, owner of the Dallas Mavericks professional basketball team, who wants to hear what his fans and season ticket-holders are thinking about. He posts his email address on the team's website and personally responds to every email.

Many hotels not only have forms in rooms, but will send an email to a guest several days later asking for feedback. Many use on line services for this and will have an appropriate "thank you" at the end of the survey.

Many restaurants will include a form with the bill for guests to complete.

It not only is important for management to review the forms but to take appropriate customer service action as suggested.

"If you give customers a chance to talk, and if you're willing to listen, they'll tell you exactly what's important to them," says Carl Sewell. "Don't guess about what they want." When they pay their service bill, customers are asked to fill out a short survey with three questions making it quick and easy for people to complete. "Present surveys in such a way customers can ignore them," Sewell says. He also conducts focus groups.[85]

Crystal Cruise Lines asks passengers to complete a questionnaire at the end of each voyage. Gregg L. Michel, president and

CEO, reads a report summary of every cruise with a tabulation of the questionnaires and sometimes reads individual comments. He also reads every letter addressed to him from a guest, and although he does not necessarily respond to each personally, a senior member of his staff does. He is probably more hands-on and connected than most travel industry executives.

The Ultimate Texas Hold'em Game in the casino of Crystal ships was implemented from an idea that originated from the questionnaires. A land program was developed in 2008 based on a letter from a guest. Another guest suggested in a letter that the spa and gym attendants continuously sanitize the fitness equipment and provide personal service with towels and water bottles, which was done.

One executive who does an exemplary job of thanking his customers is Charles A. Robertson, president, chairman and CEO of American Cruise Lines. When I took their cruise on the Snake and Columbia Rivers I was asked to complete a survey left in my cabin which I did. A month later I received a personal "thank you" from Robertson. "I read every comment card returned as I truly appreciate the time you took to send it back," he wrote. Unlike many CEOs in corporate American today, he included all personal contact information on his letterhead. His closing paragraph was: "Should you choose to sail with American Cruise Lines again and need any special assistance, please do not hesitate to contact me personally."

One CEO who should follow the lead of Robertson is Torstein Hagen, chairman and CEO of Viking River Cruises. In response to a letter I sent him, I received an unsigned, anonymous email from Viking that said: "… at this time, and in perpetuity, he [Hagen] will not accept direct contact from passengers or solicitors." Perpetuity can be a long time.

The Watchdogs

When a customer has been treated badly there are numerous ways to vent anger and seek help – social media; Internet blogs; federal, state and local government regulatory and oversight agencies; the

Better Business Bureau, and the media. Almost every television station today has a consumer advocate. Customers have scores of places to seek help.

The last thing any company, organization, institution or individual wants is for a complaint to go public or to have to respond to a government regulatory or oversight agency. The alternative to providing good customer service is an expensive involvement of lawyers and public relations crisis counselors.

In 2012 the nation lost one of its toughest watchdogs in Mike Wallace of *60 Minutes*. Because he loved taking on the big guy to help the little guy he became an investigate television legend. With budget reductions and major cutbacks in news staffs at television stations, newspapers and magazines, there are few investigative reporters or journalists today that are given the time to develop exposé stories.

Any manager or executive responsible for customer service should be aware of Consumer Action and want to have the organization as an advocate and not an adversary. Since it was founded in 1971, this nonprofit has championed consumer rights. Headquartered in San Francisco, the organization, which promotes financial literacy and economic justice, advocates consumer rights in both the media and before lawmakers. It has the resources to reach millions of consumers.

Consumer Action (www.consumer-action.org) has a comprehensive help desk that provides a free "How To Complain" booklet complete with sample letters; newsletters on class action lawsuits; a monthly on-line newsletter and a handbook complete with FAQs. Consumers who call its complaint hotline, 415-777-9635, will find speakers fluent in English, Spanish and Chinese.

There are numerous other sites on the Internet where people can seek help and comment about poor customer service. Here are just a few:

- www.complaints.com is a free site for all visitors and the entire content of email messages it receives are posted to its website. The complaints are indexed by Google, Yahoo and other search engines.

- www.thesqueakywheel.com has a one-time $5 charge per complaint which is added to the five biggest Internet search engines. It designs a complaint webpage and sends e-mails to the company you have a complaint against every time the page is viewed.
- www.econsumer.gov is a consumer database maintained by the U.S. Federal Trade Commission. There are 13 participating countries and complaint information is shared with participating consumer protection law enforcers.

Anyone involved with financial products and services needs to be familiar with the Consumer Financial Protection Bureau (www.consumerfinance.gov), a federal consumer protection agency where people can submit a complaint, tell a story and get answers to questions. Like many other services connected to the Internet, it links its messages to both Twitter and Facebook. Additionally, there are a number of websites and blogs just for angry cruise line passengers.

In most states there is a consumer protection agency or department under the supervision of the attorney general. Through the National Association of State Attorneys General (www.naag.org) consumers can find contact information for their particular state. Most have a complaint form than can be completed and submitted on-line.

Every customer service and crisis management plan should include detailed information about organizations that could become involved in a complaint related to its product and service.

Endnotes

[55] Lou Holtz, *Winning Every Day*, HarperBusiness, A division of HarperCollins Publisher, New York, N.Y., 1998.

[56] Associated Press, "Rude employees cost McDonald's millions," July 11, 2001.

57 Chris Cassatt, *Shoe*, December 29, 2007.

58 Associated Press, "Call this customer service? Hey, it's New York," December 30, 2002.

59 Sonal Rupani, "I hear America griping," *Business Week*, March 5, 2007.

60 Matt Crenson, Associated Press, "We're rude, we're crude – hey, like it or lump it," April 3, 2002.

61 Jena McGregor, "Customer Service Champs," "Rebel With A Stalled Cause," and "Consumer Vigilantes," *Business Week*, March 3, 2008, pgs. 037-052.

62 Ibid.

63 Carl Sewell and Paul B. Brown, op.cit.

64 Ibid.

65 Interview with Jim Ukrop, February 21, 2013.

66 "100% Satisfaction Guarantee Workbook," Hampton Inn/Hampton Inn & Suites.

67 David Cabela, *op.cit.*, pg. 19.

68 Sam Walton, op.cit.

69 Avery Comarow, "Broken? No problem," *U.S. News & World Report*, January 11, 1999, pg. 68.

70 Bruce Weinstein, Ph.D., "The Ethics of Outsourcing Customer Service," *Bloomberg Businessweek,* September 27, 2007.

71 Michael Arndt, "Keeping Customers Happy," *Bloomberg Businessweek*, February 18, 2010.

72 Clernie Nye, "The Advantages of Outsourcing Customer Service," eHow, www.ehow.com.

73 Luke Arthur, "Disadvantage of Outsourcing Customer Service, eHow, www.ehow.com.

74 Bruce Weinstein, Ph.D., op.cit.

75 Reuters, "Sprint ditches customers who complain too much," July 9, 2007; Associated Press, "Sprint disconnects customers who complain too much," *USA Today*, July 9, 2007; E-mail to author from Roni Singleton, public relations manager corporate communications, Sprint Nextel, Atlanta, Georgia, July 10, 2007; Rene A. Henry, "The Customer Service Oxymoron," odwyerpr.com, July 11, 2007; Spencer E. Ante, "Sprint's Wake-Up Call," *Business Week*, March 3, 2008, pg. 054.

76 Corby Kummer, "Tyranny – It's What's For Dinner," *Vanity Fair*, February 2013, pgs. 80-85.

77 Ibid.

78 Corby Kummer, op.cit.

79 Wikipedia

80 Corby Kummer, op.cit.

81 "Celebrity Chefs on Service," Patachou, Inc. Blog, July 27, 2012.

82 Corby Kummer, op.cit.

83 Ann Zimmerman, "Can This Former Clerk Save Best Buy,?" *The Wall Street Journal*, April 26, 2013, pg. B1.

84 Ibid., pg. B6.

85 Carl Sewell and Paul B. Brown, op.cit.

Chapter VI

The Gate Guardians

The people who are hired to help the boss sometimes can be the source of serious problems. Gate guardians who keep a wall around the CEO and want to know everything about the caller, themselves have been responsible for crises.

Gate guardians may have cost Landor Associates, an internationally prominent design and brand-consulting firm based in San Francisco, the opportunity to do a major corporate identity and logo program for the George H. W. Bush Presidential Library and Museum. When I was executive director of university relations at Texas A&M University, where the presidential library was to be sited, was organizing the names of several firms to be considered for the project.

When I lived in San Francisco I was well aware of the firm's reputation and attended several special events on board a renovated ferry boat that served as the company's offices. But some 25 years later, when I called to get current information about the firm – a capabilities statement and client list – I was rebuffed by both the switchboard operator and an overly officious secretary.

Both guarded their management so well that I could not speak to anyone in authority. The palace guards demanded to know everything there was to know about the project which I could not reveal.

Frustrated, I gave them my name, title and affiliation and urged the secretary to please give it to her boss.

I gave the library's director complete information packages on several design firms that I recommended. No one ever returned my call and no information on Landor Associates' qualifications and experience was received. Today, most of the information I requested can easily be accessed on the Internet.

Know Your Boss

Gate guards need to listen carefully to the caller. Donald Keough, former president of Coca-Cola and now chairman of the board of Allen & Company, New York investment banking firm, told the following story to *Leaders* magazine: "I called one of my associates at Coca-Cola and said, 'This is Don Keough, I'd like to speak to (name of individual).' The secretary on the other end of the line said, 'Who is this?' I replied, 'Don Keough.' And she asked, 'How do you spell that?' I said K-e-o-u-g-h. And then she wanted to know 'What business are you in?' I told her 'I work for The Coca-Cola Company.' She said she would try to get her boss to call me back at a later date." Keough never said if the secretary continued to work for Coca-Cola.

There is one gate guardian whose face I would have loved to have seen when I had a perfect reply for her. I called her boss, the chairman of a major *Fortune* 500 company and one of the country's major philanthropists, and said: "Hello, this is Rene Henry. Is (name) available?" She replied, "Does he know you, Mr. Henry?" I said, "Yes, we've been friends for 25 years."

That wasn't sufficient for her. "Who do you work for, Mr. Henry?" At the time, I was immersed in the 1988 George H. W. Bush presidential campaign organizing all of the athletes and entertainers, so I just answered, "The Vice President." Her voice was so cold it would have frozen water if I had a glass in my hand, when she curtly asked, "the vice president of what?" I couldn't resist, and almost laughing, understated, "The United States of America." There was absolute silence. Within five seconds my friend was on the phone, "Rene, how are you? ...."

When management consultant and author Tom Peters called 13 firms to pose a basic question or to file a complaint, his research turned up everything from great service to being rudely disconnected. Peters called Yoplait and wanted to know the yogurt maker's stance on bovine growth hormones, and the operator refused to transfer the call to anyone. At Ben & Jerry's his same question brought a swift transfer to the public relations department and an eight-minute discussion on why the ice cream maker shuns the additive.

He called IBM to request an annual report and information regarding the annual meeting. He was transferred to stockholder relations and an enthusiastic operator gave way to a disinterested voice recording and he left a message. The information he wanted arrived two weeks after the annual meeting.[86]

When Peters called General Motors to ask why it was taking automakers so long to develop electric cars, his request to speak with CEO Jack Smith was denied. He was transferred to the library, then to a non-working number, then disconnected. When he called Nordstrom and asked to speak to the CEO about a problem in the shoe department, just one transfer later CEO Bruce Nordstrom was on the line. He listened patiently and promised to fix the problem.[87]

Getting Around the Gate Guards

Sometimes it's fun to give the gate guardians some of their own medicine. With creativity, ingenuity and networking, often you can find a way to get around them.

When I was director of communications and government relations for the mid-Atlantic States region of the U.S. Environmental Protection Agency, I decided to use quotes in our annual report from famous people who were either born and raised or who had successful careers in the region.

Working with my staff team, we developed a priority list. As I expected, the publicity flacks for some entertainment and sports stars either turned us down or never responded. How could someone in the public eye not support the environment?

After not being able to get through to one actor, I learned that his father was a prominent Philadelphia architect, planner and environmental champion. I asked him to please deliver my request to his son. In a matter of days I had a great quote. For an Olympic champion, I got her quote by going through her father. For news anchors and personalities at CBS and NBC, I had friends at both networks put my requests in the interoffice mail. For a couple of others I went through mutual friends. The annual report was a success.

Sometimes you even have to circumvent your own partner. I co-founded ICPR public relations in 1975 and I was having lunch with one of my partners, Mort Segal, at the Beverly Wilshire Hotel. A woman who was a mover-and-shaker in Los Angeles came over to our table and asked us for help. "Carol Burnett has always supported our charity financially and in anyway we have ever asked," she said. "I've left word several times with the secretary of one of your partners and he has not called me back."

After lunch and back at our office, Mort said, "I'm going to call Carol." Burnett said she would love to help by doing several public service television commercials and that was her favorite charity. Two hours later when Mort and I were in a staff meeting our partner, Rick, angrily broke in. He had represented her for years and more often than not always turned down such requests without ever asking his client. After he had vented and began to calm down, Mort reminded him that he would have said "No" and probably had no idea it was one of Carol's favorite charities and in fact, the result ended up making two women very happy.

Just Ask the Mayor

All too often you have to get accustomed to people not being responsive and have to overcome all types of obstacles in order to accomplish your objectives. An overzealous gate guard in Mayor Ed Koch's office almost cost New York City the opportunity of being part of a major event that honored the 1984 U.S. Olympic medal winners.

This special event was not only the most logistically challenging but rewarding project in my career. It was the week-long "Tribute to Achievement" tour of the 1984 U.S. Olympic medal winners. Underwritten by the Southland Corporation, owners of 7-Eleven, every U.S. medal winner and a guest were invited to participate. The tour with 250 Olympians began Monday morning, August 13 with a breakfast in Los Angeles with President and Mrs. Ronald Reagan. Following were stops in Washington, D.C. for an event at The Capitol, then to New York, a stop at Disneyworld in Orlando, and a finale with a parade in Dallas and barbeque at South Fork Ranch.

For weeks my partner in New York, Don Smith, had tried to get an answer from a woman in Mayor Koch's office who was responsible for special events including parades. She gave him every excuse not to provide an answer, including demanding a guarantee of how many New York City Olympians would win medals. We predicted two, both African-Americans – Mark Breland in boxing and Peter Westbrook in fencing. Both did medal.

Finally we reached the decision day. Our backup to New York was Chicago. Don and I believed the woman never discussed the parade with Mayor Koch, and used him as an excuse for not giving an answer. We felt the best time to bring this to the mayor's attention would be on a weekend and when he was not at his office. We networked our relationships to get our message to him.

Don called Sonny Werbelin, the late sports and entertainment impresario, and good friend of Koch. He called Koch at home and asked him why he didn't want a ticker-tape parade to honor the U.S. medal winners. I called Bill Simon, our first Energy Czar, former Secretary of the Treasury and a Wall Street heavyweight, who also was a close friend of Koch. Simon also was president of the U.S. Olympic Committee. He also called the mayor at home. As we expected, Koch knew nothing of our request and thought it was an absolutely fantastic idea. He also didn't appreciate being made the "heavy" in the situation by one of staff members.

During his Monday morning staff meeting Koch expressed his outrage with his appointee. Of course New York was ready to roll out the red carpet for the Olympians. Later in the week I received a call from the young woman who started talking down to me, cursed me, and threatened me to "never ever do that again." I told her not to worry because I had a direct line to the mayor and she would never have to worry about ever returning any of my future phone calls.

More than two-and-one-half million people lined Broadway to salute the Olympians as Koch led the ticker-tape parade, the largest in New York history until the one honoring the veterans returning from Desert Storm.

Endnotes

[86] Ellen Neuborne, *USA Today*, Section B, Pg. 1, May 10, 1994.

[87] Ibid.

[88] Jeffrey L. Rodengen, *A Century of Service 1907-2007Amica*, 2007, Write Stuff Enterprises, Inc., Ft. Lauderdale, Florida

PART II

Successful Case Histories

Chapter VII

Amica Mutual Insurance Co.

Amica Mutual Insurance Company was founded in 1907 in Providence, Rhode Island as Automobile Mutual Insurance Company of America with an ironclad commitment to customer service. Employees and policyholder-customers soon began to call the new company by its acronym, "Amica." In 1973 it became the official company name.

During World War II the company served as a fiduciary agent of the War Damage Corporation and insured the homes of policyholders against damage from enemy combatants. Automobile coverage, however, represented 98 percent of Amica's business.

Since, Amica has expanded its business to all types of residential property and casualty insurance, boat insurance, umbrella liability insurance and even life insurance.

Adolph Thomas Vigneron, founded Amica as a mutual company owned by its policyholders instead of stockholders. He relied on growth of the company exclusively on personal referrals from existing policyholders rather than through soliciting agents. He believed that each policyholder would be responsible for the success of the company as a whole and would only recommend other prudent people to the company. Each year policyholders received a dividend based on a percentage of their premium and company profits. This lowered the overall cost of insurance and was an incentive for them to recommend only desirable, low-risk acquaintances to Amica. The core of his business philosophy was to provide exceptional customer service.[88]

Amica's underwriters have always been paid a salary instead of a commission. From a one-room business with two clerks it has grown to a staff or more than 3,000. Vince Burks, senior assistant vice president and communications director, attributes the company's success to its dedicated employees. "In October 2012, nearly 30 percent of our employees had been with Amica for 20 or more years. This has translated to a policyholder retention rate of 93.62 percent. More than half of our customers have been with Amica for 10 years or longer and nearly one-third for 20 years or more."

I have been an Amica customer and policyholder since 1958 when I insured my automobile with them. I have since added homeowners and umbrella coverage policies and when I owned a sailboat, Amica protected it as well.

The company has been honored time and again for its outstanding customer service. Since 1962, *Consumer Reports* has given Amica its #1 score for automobile and homeowners insurance companies 18 times. In 2006, the company received the "Highest Customer Satisfaction Among National Auto Insurers" award from J.D. Power Associates for the seventh straight year. Also in 2006, J.D. Power awarded Amica "Highest Customer Satisfaction Among National Homeowner Insurers" for the fifth consecutive year. By 2012, Amica had received a total of 11 consecutive homeowner awards and 13 consecutive auto awards from J.D. Power.

During Amica's 85th anniversary in 1992, the U.S. suffered devastating tornadoes, Hurricane Andrew, and the most powerful Northeast coastal storm of the century. It was catastrophic for property and casualty insurers. The industry had record-breaking losses of $16.5 billion, Amica received glowing reviews for the way it serviced its policyholders who had losses. And, it continued to reward all with dividends.

A tribute to the success of its customer service is Amica's

limited advertising until the 1990's. The company grew through word-of-mouth and referrals. You could not even find Amica listed in the Yellow Pages. Management believed it was important to use radio and television advertising in areas where it did not yet have an established presence. The first television commercials debuted in 1998. Before the campaign, Amica was the #1 company in the country for service that no one had ever heard of.

"Successful companies know how to run successful businesses," says Burks. "They know how to win over and keep customers. They know how to hire and inspire their workforces. They know the importance of giving 100 percent. They know lagniappe.

"Lagniappe means an added emphasis on customer service. Extra courteous. Extra responsive. Always available. Our employees proactively reach out to our clients. They listen to them carefully, patiently, and thoroughly. They treat them well. They build trust."

Burks says lagniappe in Spanish means special and notes that Mark Twain, during his travels in New Orleans, explained "It is the equivalent of the 13th roll in a 'baker's dozen' … something thrown in, gratis, for good measure."

"The concept of lagniappe is not just a part of our brand ethos," he says, "It is ingrained in everything we do. It therefore extends to our most valued resource – our employees. In fact, that is the secret to our success."[89]

Until 1941 Amica had only one office – its Providence headquarters. It opened its first branch in Boston later that year. Expansion plans were put on hold until the end of World War II and a second office was opened in Springfield, Massachusetts in 1946. In 1949, the San Francisco branch was opened and by the mid-1950s, more than 24 branch offices were bringing the company even closer to its policyholders. By 2006, 38 branch offices served customers throughout the country. Assets grew from less than $14,000 in 1907 to more than $4 billion by 2012.

Since 1994 Michael Fineman, president of San Francisco-based Fineman PR, has compiled an "Annual Top 10 PR Blunders List." In 2012 two insurance companies made his list – Liberty Mutual and Progressive.

A plaintiff whose sister was insured by Progressive and who died in a 2010 traffic accident was startled in court to see a Progressive lawyer assisting the defense in an attempt to undermine his family's claim on his sister's policy. Fineman said that CNN Money reported that Progressive "didn't handle social media replies well" including a clipped, repetitive tweet instead of apologizing to the family. Fineman added that according to *The Wall Street Journal* more than 1,000 Twitter users dropped Progressive.[90]

To make Fineman's list, Liberty Mutual, headquartered in Boston, was under scrutiny from the Massachusetts Division of Insurance after it was discovered that Edmund F. "Ted" Kelly, the longtime CEO, earned an average of $50 million a year from 2008 to 2010. A story in the *Boston Globe* revealed that the company also spent $4.5 million in 2011 to renovate a 1,315 square foot office suite for income CEO David Long that included woven silk wall coverings, a private shower, exercise room and an automatic lighting system. Management disregarded the fact that as a mutual company extra profits should be returned to the policyholders and not the executives. Liberty Mutual did not issue a single statement of regret after stories in the *Boston Globe*. Kelly explained his pay as "an accounting issue."[91]

Endnotes

[89] Vince Burks, op.cit.

[90] "Top 10 PR Blunders of 2012," December 17, 2012, Fineman PR, San Francisco, www.finemanpr.com.

[91] Ibid.

Chapter VIII

Marriott Hotels

In May 1927, J. Willard and Alice Sheets Marriott opened a small A&W root beer stand in downtown Washington, D.C. It was later renamed The Hot Shoppe. Until it opened two motels in the 1950s, the company was in the food service business and known as a regional family restaurant chain.

From its humble beginnings, the one root beer stand has grown to an international lodging company with more than 300,000 associates (what Marriott calls its employees) in 3,700 managed and franchised properties in 74 countries. The company has more than a dozen brands of hotels and resorts ranging from Courtyard, Springhill Suites and Fairfield Inn & Suites for the budget-minded to its luxury J.W. Marriott, Renaissance and Ritz-Carlton hotels.

In 1978 Marriott revolutionized its business approach by focusing on being a hotel management company rather than a hotel ownership company. Properties were sold to real estate investors with long-term management contracts. The company gained more financial flexibility by not being hamstrung by mortgages and debt. This launched Marriott into a growth era to become one of the world's major real estate developers.

The company is consistently honored for its outstanding customer service and *Fortune* magazine has named it on its "100 Best

Companies to Work For" list every year since the list began in 1998. Britain's *The Sunday Times* voted Marriott the fourth best company to work for in the U.K. "One of our core values that has been our company credo since my parents' era is 'Take care of your employees, and they'll take care of your customers.' We put our people first," said J. Willard "Bill" Marriott, Jr., who began his career by washing pots in the kitchen when he was a student at the University of Utah. He joined the company in 1956, became president in 1964, and now is executive chairman and chairman of the board.

"The other four fundamental principles – powerful aspirations that are easy to remember but challenging to live up to are: act with integrity; pursue excellence; embrace change; and serve our world," Marriott adds. "Our culture results in measurably lower employee turnover and higher customer satisfaction."[92]

Bill Marriott also is a strong believer in management-by-walking-around. "A manager who doesn't know his staff by name, who doesn't spend the bulk of the day walking the heart of the house, will eventually have problems," he says. "He's not going to have the same rapport with associates or the knowledge base to make decisions as do his more engaged counterparts.

"This has been our policy since the moment my parents opened the doors of their first root beer stand. My father was the ultimate hands-on manager. I expect our general managers to get out of their offices as much as possible. Companies that get into trouble are the ones where the CEO never budges from the executive suite."[93]

"We listen to our associates. That is how you empower people to grow in their jobs and gain confidence as decision makers," Marriott says. "Many of our associates are 'cross-trained' and teamwork is a hallmark of our corporate culture. Customers aren't going to hear 'That's not my job' from anyone at Marriott."

Filling Rooms On Weekends

As Marriott began to grow in the hotel business it faced the same challenge as all of its competitors – hotels with scores of empty rooms on weekends. When he played and coached for the Washington Redskins, Sam Huff, the Hall of Fame linebacker, frequently drove by Marriott headquarters. In 1971 he went to the company with an idea to fill vacant hotels on weekends in major cities. From his concept, a sports division was launched.

"I started with friends in the National Football League, expanded it to college teams, the officials and the media that covered the game, and of course the fans followed," Huff says. "They all wanted to be near the team."

"I worked with the business managers of the teams. We had a sales person in every hotel who became a sports rep who looked after everything our sports customers wanted," he added. "We soon expanded into other sports – baseball, the professional golf tour, and overnight Marriott was #1 in sports. Soon, new hotels were being built on the West Coast and we immediately knew they could sell out on weekends with the sports business."[94]

Huff retired as vice president in 1998. The division has since had a number of iterations. After nearly 10 years with Marriott, in 2007 Randy Griffin was named vice president of sales for corporate, government, affinity and entertainment. "In addition to sports we now look for other opportunities that include multi-cultural, military, family and school reunions; the wedding market; and layer in different types of businesses," Griffin says.

Since the beginning of the sports division in the early 1970s, Marriott's weekend occupancy has led all competitors. The company now exclusively represents the U.S. national governing bodies of nine amateur and Olympic sports, is the official lodging partner for the National Football League and U.S. Golf, and has strong marketing partnerships with all major sports organizations.[95]

Making That Extra Effort

In his new book, Bill Marriott cites a number of examples how associates made an extra effort to help a guest. When some survivors of the airplane Capt. "Sully" Sullenberger landed in the Hudson River showed up cold, wet and barefoot at the New York Marriott Marquis, front desk associates got petty cash and ran to a local sporting goods store to buy them sweatpants, sweatshirts, socks and sneakers.

A laundry attendant in Texas once spent two hours helping a guest who was in double arm casts do her hair and makeup, brush her teeth and do her shoes so she could be on time to see her son play in a championship soccer game.

A hotel general manager went so far as to go diving in a garbage dumpster to retrieve the dental retainer of a young guest. Other associates have loaned jewelry, coats, blouses and other items to guests who forgot to pack them. One was a suit for a guest whose luggage was missing and needed for a critical job interview. And another gave a pair of shoes to a guest who forgot to pack dress shoes for an important meeting.

"Successful companies are about more than simply making money," Marriott writes. "We can empower individuals and help build stable communities at a time when many of our traditional social institutions are struggling with shrinking budgets. He cites the company's social responsibility when Hurricane Katrina hit New Orleans in August 2005. "Three of our hotels were flooded and eight others felt the impact. As usual, associates donated money and personal leave time. They, along with the company, our family, and business partners raised more than $5 million for associate assistance and volunteered over five years to help rebuild homes, schools and playgrounds.

"After a severe earthquake hit China's Sichuan Province in May 2008, one of our general managers led her hotel team in raising money, and including owners' donations, our contribution was more than $3 million."

Know Your Customers

Marriott says it is important to give visitors to the U.S. the kind of gracious welcome Americans love to receive when visiting an unfamiliar place, including being greeted in your language, see a familiar item on a menu or be able to see a favorite program or sports team on television.

Li Yu, which means "Serve With Courtesy" in Mandarin, is the name of the special welcome program for Chinese guests. When they arrive they are greeted by a Mandarin-speaking associate. Chinese newspapers, television programs, tea, popular Chinese condiments, and favorite foods are available. Another touch is the assignment of rooms and floors that include the numbers six and eight which are considered auspicious in the Chinese culture.

Sharon Van Vechten, fashion and hospitality industry consultant, speaking from first-hand experience, praises the company for its Marriott Vacation Club. "They do an amazing job the way they reward and engage the time share owners."

Marriott started its Honored Guest Awards program in 1983 and combined several incentives into Marriott Rewards that now has more than 40 million members.

Over the years I've stayed at scores of Marriott hotels in the U.S. and overseas and for meetings and special events for clients. Bill Marriott's new book is one of the best down-to-earth, common sense books on management that I have read.

Endnotes

[92] J.W. Marriott, Jr. and Kathi Ann Brown, *Without Reservations – How A Family Root Beer Stand Grew Into a Global Hotel Company*, Luxury Custom Publishing, San Diego, 2013.

[93] Ibid.

[94] Interviews with Sam Huff, January-February 2013.

[95] Interview with Randy Griffin, February 5, 2013.

Chapter IX

Crystal Cruise Lines

More people are taking cruises today than ever before – more than 15 million in 2010 according to Cruise Lines International Association, a prediction of 16 million in 2011.[96]

But all cruises are not like the television series' *Love Boat*. Between 1995 and 2012, an alarming number of more than 165 passengers have gone missing from cruise ships. Some died, fell or jumped overboard, or just disappeared without any explanation.[97]

In recent years some cruise ships have run aground, hit icebergs, and even sunk. Engine room fires, boiler explosions and mechanical problems have forced ships to skip ports of call and create arrival delays, causing passengers to miss return home flight connections. Even worse, some have floated at sea for days with no power, running water, air conditioning, toilet or sanitary facilities or food service.

Additionally there have been reports of rape and assault. Outbreaks of Norwalk Virus, also called Norovirus, and other illnesses, have ruined cruises for hundreds more. Passengers have been seriously injured, or died, on shore excursions.

For years cruise lines have deceived consumers with regard to pricing. In more than 200 articles he has written, Thomas A. Dickerson, a justice of the Supreme Court of the State of New York, cites scores of lawsuits against cruise lines involving false, misleading and deceptive advertising.

Even though the world's two largest cruise lines are headquartered in Miami – Carnival Corporation and Royal Caribbean Ltd. – there is little recourse for passengers because most ships are registered in a foreign country, fly foreign flags and are not subject to regulation. The Department of Transportation could easily create a database to list all incidents regarding cruise ships. The thought of having such a website for consumers to check should be supported by the cruise lines, but would be fiercely opposed.

There are numerous blogs and websites on the Internet where passengers list the problems they have on a cruise. Almost every complaint you can imagine has been made by unhappy passengers: misleading advertising; misrepresentation of promotional items; poor or cold food; poor and rude service; dirty staterooms; cancelled excursions; itinerary and venue changes; food poisoning; thefts from staterooms; lack of supervision for children; dirty swimming pools; bait-and-switch tactics; no special attention for disabled passengers; being "nickel and dimed" for incidental items; lack of regular housekeeping; bed bugs on blankets; noisy, rowdy and drunk passengers; no followup on complaints; lost luggage; and lack of professional medical attention, equipment, and facilities.

The $25 billion-a-year cruise industry has had to deal with countless lawsuits, including 2,100 in South Florida alone in 2001. Most lawsuits are filed by a small group of lawyers in the Miami area who specialize in maritime law.[98]

The cruise lines are lawyered-up and spend millions to lobby their special interests so do not expect any consumer protection legislation or regulation from Congress. From 2008-2012, the Cruise Line International Association spent $8.562 million and Royal Caribbean $6.847 million on lobbying. This does not include money given directly to members of Congress, PACs or Super PACs or rerouted through law firms.

Listening and Anticipating = #1

A shining star in the industry is Crystal Cruise Lines. Headquartered in Los Angeles. Crystal is consistently ranked #1 in its category for cruise ships. The philosophy of Gregg L. Michel, its president, is to listen and anticipate. For 17 consecutive years Crystal has been voted the "World's Best Large Ship Cruise Line" by the readers of *Travel+Leisure* magazine, and is the only cruise line, hotel or resort to be voted "World's Best" that many times in the magazine's history.

Several years ago, following 30 days on the Crystal Symphony, I disembarked at Civitavecchia, Italy, the coastal port for Rome. All cruise ships have transportation from the port generally to a central station where tourists can take taxis to their hotels or trains to other cities. We heard rumors of a taxi driver strike in Rome, which was confirmed by the hostess on our bus. She immediately alleviated our concerns when she told us that Crystal was taking us to another location where vans had been reserved to take us to our preferred locations.

In keeping with Crystal's exemplary customer service, the hostess said there would not be any charge for this service and Crystal had taken care of all gratuities. She further apologized for any inconvenience. During the next several days in Rome, I met people who had been on other cruises who had to find their own solution to the taxi strike. One couple said their cruise line dropped them at the central point without any warning of the strike. They felt they were fortunate to find a gypsy driver who took them to their hotel even though they were charged 10 times the normal rate. Another couple was not as fortunate and had to walk nearly two miles pulling their bags on wheels. Crystal did not want its passengers inconvenienced in anyway, much less stranded, and anticipated and did what had to be done. This is extraordinary customer service.

Michel's mission is to be the best in luxury service, not just in the cruise industry. "For warm and gracious service to be authentic, you need truly nice people," says Michel. "So we hire people whose parents raised them right. Everyone needs to be treated with respect, including our colleagues."

As a further convenience to guests, Michel implemented early embarkation on Crystal ships with a complimentary lunch, and a service to check hand-carry luggage before guests' rooms are ready. Each year he hosts a President's Cruise and spends a few days visiting every annual World Cruise. He likes to meet with guests individually, and conducts a public question and answer forum open to all passengers. Crystal also conducts on-going research with guests through focus groups or quantitative studies.

Michel hosts an Awards Gala for his top producing travel agents each year. During the several days of seminars for agents, he schedules meeting times where the agents share their clients' positive and negative feedback. He also has been very aggressive in establishing and maintaining environmental "green" standards on all ships.

Responding to Problems Beyond Its Control

When you have a team prepared to respond, crises can be resolved quickly, even when not anticipated. This happened to Crystal on October 26, 2005 when the Crystal Serenity was headed for Barcelona, only to learn that striking Spanish fisherman had blockaded the harbor. To keep on schedule, Crystal hoped to go to Port Vendres, but the alternate port could not accommodate the ship's needs. The Serenity anchored in Barcelona harbor during continuing negotiations between the government and fisherman, and after much deliberation, sailed to Gibraltar.

Guests scheduled to board in Barcelona were accommodated in hotels there for two nights, and then flown to Malaga, an hour from the port. Because of a political situation involving Gibraltar and Spain, there was no direct flight from Barcelona to Gibraltar. Passengers were given free hotel accommodations and meals, reimbursed for two days lost on the cruise, given $200 credit for a future cruise, and free Internet access for two days to contact family and friends.

Departing passengers were flown back to Barcelona and re-accommodated with complimentary rooms and meals, and transfers from the hotel to the airport. Guests who made their own air travel arrangements were given travel assistance. Travel agents with guests on board were faxed, and all passengers onboard, and in Barcelona, received communications throughout the two day ordeal. The cost to Crystal was more than $2 million.

On a cruise, no one ever wants to miss a scheduled port. However, it does happen sometimes when bad weather, wind and high waves would endanger the safety of passengers who would be tendered to shore – taken in lifeboats from the ship anchored in a harbor. Weather generally is no problem when the ship has a dock.

Jaque Brown, an on-board Crystal Society hostess, recalls a fellow crew member speaking of weather impacting two ports on one cruise. "Our shore excursion and front desk staff were swamped with complaints and somewhat upset guests. The staff did their best to explain, apologize and make amends," she says.

"When Captain Zander learned that the front desk and shore excursion staff had become the target, he apologized over the public address system and announced that he would be at the front desk in 10 minutes to personally listen to any guest concerns regarding the issue – and he was." This is another example of why customer service must start at the top.

Doing it right helps you be #1.

Endnotes

[96] Cruise Lines International Association, www.cruising.org, January 13, 2011.

[97] Natalie Clarke, Mail Online, *Daily Mail*, London, England, September 23, 2011.

[98] Amy Martinez, "Lawyers turn cruise lawsuits into industry," *The Miami Herald*.

Chapter X

The Washington Nationals: Filling Empty Seats

Promoters and organizers and those responsible for all types of special events should give the unsold tickets to their events to the USO and organizations that serve youth, active military and their families, and those financially unable to purchase tickets. Filling what could be empty seats with those who might not otherwise be able to afford to buy a ticket not only creates goodwill and builds customer service but it is smart business and the right thing to do. Empty seats also translate to lost sales at the concession stands.

Many college and professional teams have policies in place to give someone an opportunity to see a sports event that otherwise might not be affordable. It is an inexpensive way to build a loyal fan base. For colleges, in the long run, it might even make the difference of one day getting a top recruit.

When an event is televised and the camera shows empty seats it impacts on the image of the event or home team. You will never see an empty seat when Oscars are presented by the Academy of Motion Picture Arts & Sciences or Emmys by the Academy of Television Arts & Sciences. Once a recipient is honored and goes to the stage a "sitter" immediately takes his or her place until s/he can return later during the event.

The Washington Nationals major league baseball team has an outstanding community relations and customer service program. Through the USO it provides free tickets for active military and their families as well as various youth organizations throughout the metropolitan area, Maryland and Northern Virginia. In addition to giving away free tickets, the Nationals have a youth baseball academy, participate with numerous charitable organizations and even have a pediatric diabetes care complex at Children's National Medical Center.

"Through its extraordinary support of USO-Metro, the Nats continue to hit one grand slam after another when it comes to supporting our military members and their families," said Elaine Rogers, president and CEO of USO of Metropolitan Washington, D.C. USO-Metro honored the team with its Legacy of Hope award, named after Bob Hope. The sold-out, black-tie dinner had more than 500 guests and raised $630,000.

Few professional teams are as involved with their communities as the Nationals. Several of its programs are being adapted by other teams and USO chapters in other geographic regions of the country. It's "Me and a Friend" program allows children of military families to bring a friend free to a game. It has a Wounded Warrior Amputee softball team and members of the Nationals make regular vists to military hospitals.

The Los Angeles Lakers sell out most of their home games but still give away at least 100 tickets to every game to nonprofit groups serving children and the military. According to John Black, vice president, the value of the tickets during a season is nearly $200,000.

According to Greg Aielo, vice president of the National Football League, each of the 32 teams can give away up to 17,000 complimentary tickets during a season.

Sports events are only one area where promoters and organizers build goodwill with free tickets. Broadway Theatres have had a policy for years. Some even provide the USO with free standing room tickets at sold out shows.

When you think of a baseball "ball boy" you think of someone who is a teenager or younger and today of equal gender. The San Francisco Giants have added a new dimension and now have senior citizens filling this duty. The Giants trained 70 men (called balldudes) and 20 women (called balldudettes) for their roles during games. Some hopefuls pay up to $500 to attend Giants' Balldude Camp to shag pop-ups and grounders and answer trivia questions as well as sit on stools while batters hit grounders down the line to them. Most are more than 60 years old and some over 70. They are paid $15 a game for each of three of four games they work each season.

When the sales and marketing team fails to sell out a game or event the unsold tickets should be given to the public relations professionals who will make sure there are no empty seats

Chapter XI

Government Customer Service

Federal, state and local governments all talk about customer service but few practice what they preach. At some government offices, customer service is an oxymoron. Today, public demands for quality service are at an all-time high, trust in government is eroding, and the public's willingness to pay for services through taxes and fees is dropping.[99]

Quality of service from a government department or agency will vary from office to office, and also from administration to administration. In 1992, when Marvin Runyon was named the 70th Postmaster General, he inherited an organization that suffered from media critics, the jokes of late night comedians, and increased violence among its workforce.

Runyon placed an emphasis on customer service, and to head communications, he hired Larry Speakes, the White House press secretary under President Ronald Reagan from 1981-1987. "To me, communications is the most important thing you do in business. If you can't communicate with your employees, your customers, your suppliers – then you're not going to do a good job," Runyon said.

During his six years heading the U.S. Postal Service, he reduced staff by 46,000, rejuvenated marketing, instilled a sprit of pride and competitiveness and converted the post office into a thriving business with three successive years of billion-dollar-plus profits.[100] In 2001, Jack Potter, a career postal employee, was named the 72nd Postmaster General. Under his management, USPS no longer communicated the way Runyon's team did, and customer service all too often was non-existent. Internet blogs suggested Congress remove "service" from the USPS name and the slogan "we deliver, we deliver" as being false advertising. An exception to this is my local East Union post office station and my letter carrier where customer service is exceptional and exceed my expectations.

Is There A Change in the Future?

The federal government is making progress and there may be hope for all of us in the future. In 2011, President Obama issued an Executive Order requiring each agency to develop plans to improve customer service. On September 11, 2012 the U.S. House of Representatives passed by a voice vote the Government Customer Service Improvement Act. A similar bill is in the Senate.

"When taxpayers interact with a government agency, they deserve the same timely, reliable assistance they would expect from a private sector business," said Rep. Henry Cuellar (D-Texas), the bill's chief sponsor. He noted that only 31 percent of people were satisfied with federal customer service. Previously, South Carolina Governor Nikki Haley directed all state employees to cheerfully answer the phone.[101]

The public can see what various agencies are doing regarding customer service by going to the following website: http://www.performance.gov/. "The American people deserve a government that is responsive to their needs. Whether they are calling the IRS for an answer to a tax question or visiting a Social Security Administration office to adjust their benefits, they should expect high-quality interactions with the federal government," the site reads. "Yet despite some important strides to improve customer service during the past 15 years, customer expectations continue to rise. The Federal Government must keep pace with the public's expectations and transform its customer services."

EPA Philadelphia - A Role Model for Governments

The mid-Atlantic States regional office of the U.S. Environmental Protection Agency in Philadelphia is a role model all government agencies should copy. The importance of personal communications skills and customer service is exemplified by the region's established policies.

"Our surveys of Congressional offices and state agencies consistently showed that prompt replies to calls and mail were much preferred to more "perfect" replies that took days or longer. Why? The survey results, and my 35 years of government experience, tell me that people value a caring attitude at least as much as the specific information provided in response to their inquires," says Lawrence Teller, the region's senior communications advisor. "Even better is knowing what people are concerned about, and letting them know what EPA knows, even before they ask. The Internet and related technologies provide the means to service this 'right to know' approach."

The office was the first EPA region that established a sizeable cash award to recognize the outstanding customer service performer each year. Here are just a few practices that were established in the mid-1990s by the region's office of communications and government relations that serve as a model for everyone:

- Respond to all phone calls before, and no later than the end of the next business day, and preferably the same day. If the individual called cannot personally respond, then an associate should follow through.
- Respond to all letters, faxes and e-mails within 72 hours. E-mails should be responded to preferably within 24 hours. Give an interim reply when there is a good reason that a complete answer is going to be delayed.
- The voice mailbox should be updated weekly and always when on travel. Many employees updated their voice mailbox daily.

- When on travel or vacation, an "out of office" response should be left for e-mails, and preferably with someone as an emergency contact.

Teller, who spearheaded customer service not only for the region, but as the lead for all EPA regions, says additional principles of the organization's customer service include several that were adopted by the agency's customer service steering committee as EPA's Six Principles of Customer Service:

- Be helpful! Listen to your customers.
- Respond to all phone calls by the end of the next business day.
- Respond to all correspondence within 10 business days. (Headquarters and the other regions would not adopt the 72-hour policy of the Philadelphia region).
- Make clear, timely, accurate information accessible.
- Work collaboratively with partners to improve all products and services.
- Involve customers and use their ideas.

FEMA and Hurricanes

It's too bad FEMA couldn't take a page out of the EPA customer service book. While touring the disaster of Hurricane Katrina in New Orleans in 2005, few will forget the widely televised compliment President George W. Bush paid Michael D. Brown, the Undersecretary of Emergency Preparedness and Response (EP&R) and head of FEMA, with an "Atta-boy-Brownie" slap on the back.

Following Hurricane Sandy in 2012 President Barack Obama pledged there would be no bureaucratic red tape. But someone forgot to tell this to FEMA staffers at one disastrous New Jersey beach town. When residents needed help the FEMA office had its doors locked and a sign that read "FEMA closed because of weather!"

At this same time, the Occupy Wall Street movement, known just as Occupy, did bring together volunteers and delivered hot meals and relief items to those in need. The Occupy leaders pointed out that 100 percent of the money raised went to the relief effort and this organization did what the bureaucracy could not.

Endnotes

[99] Tod Newcombe, "Customer Service, Government Style," *Government Technology*, October 31, 2007.

[100] "Marvelous Marvin Moves the Mail," *The Strategist*, Public Relations Society of America.

[101] Richard Simon, "Government customer service? House OKs setting standards for it," *Los Angeles Times*, September 11, 2012.

Chapter XII

Summary

A business needs to treat its employees the way it wants those employees to treat the customers who buy the company's product or service. Where applicable customer service needs to be provided for stockholders and investors.

A nonprofit organization must serve its internal audience of employees and volunteers and its external audience of those served by the organization and its donors and supporters.

A college or university is more complex and probably the one individual in all of customer service who has the largest audience to please is the person responsible for sports public relations. The campus target includes students, administration, faculty, and athletes. In addition a list includes alumni, parents, donors, media, sports fans, sponsors, and recruitable student athletes.

Customer service is really nothing more than just applying common sense to good old fashion courtesy. It is not magic. It basically is just treating your customer the way you would want to be treated. However, with today's society becoming more rude, too many people have no idea how they want to be treated. Good customer service is when you exceed the expectations of your customer, but for many businesses and organizations, the customers have no expectations.

It is a shame that customer service is not as important to a new generation of CEOs as it once was. Many companies still live on their past reputations. Never again will we see some traditions that live only in memories or books.

It was a pleasure to live in San Francisco in the Fifties and Sixties. The St. Francis Hotel had one employee whose full-time job was to polish all of the nickels, dimes, pennies, quarters and other coins. In those days women wore gloves and hats. Dan London, the hotel's owner, did not want his women guests to get dirty gloves from coins. The city's taxi drivers also would get up from behind their seats, come around the taxi and open the door for women. Can you imagine that happening today?

There is a wealth of information about customer service that anyone can retrieve on the Internet. A score of books has been written on various aspects of customer service from the philosophy of individual companies to how to train, teach and empower employees.

There is no single rule or model plan that a CEO can adapt for his company. The basic tenets that make customer service extraordinary are found in almost any plan.

The professional organization for those responsible for customer service is the Society of Consumer Affairs Professionals in Business (SOCAP International). Founded in 1973, it represents a best-in-class customer care experts across all industries worldwide. The organization is located at 625 North Washington Street, Suite 304, Alexandria, Virginia 22314, www.socap.org, phone 703-519-3700.

Another outstanding Internet source with information on virtually ever aspect of customer service is "Customer Service Reader at http://www.customerservicereader.typepad.com/. Readers will find some 30 categories listed and links to more than 40 sources.

Checklist of Basic Rules

Following is a checklist of some basic rules to consider:

Management

- Name a team to develop a plan with principles, goals and objectives.
- Have the customer service team periodically review the plan.
- Monitor what the competition is doing.
- Monitor what the employees are doing.
- Do not outsource customer service.
- Be available and reachable.
- If you personally cannot respond, ask a secretary, assistant or someone else.
- Do not use non-meaning, superfluous titles such as "executive communications."
- If a secretary or gate guardian forwards a letter or email to another party in the company to respond, then s/he should so inform the sender.
- Return every call and answer every letter, email, text and fax.
- Listen.
- Do not send one-way emails to which the recipient cannot reply.
- Leave a vacation response or reply on email that you are out of the office and not available. Sometimes is may be important to add even more information such as a backup contact or when you will be available.
- Leave an out of office message on your voicemail so someone trying to reach you knows you are not available and does not believe you are not returning his or her call.
- Fill all empty seats at sports, theatre, and other special events. Give free tickets to those who could not afford to attend.
- Know everything possible about organizations that could become involved in a complaint and include detailed information in the customer service and crisis information plan.

Employees
- Monitor what your employees are doing.
- Empower all employees to use their discretion and best judgment.
- Listen to the employees. Get their feedback.
- Interact with employees, especially those on the front lines.
- Never lie or ask an employee to lie, saying "I work in the office of the president" when the person is miles away and may have never even meet the CEO.

Customers
- Get feedback from customers and thank them when they respond.
- Use value cards and computer software to monitor buying habits and trends.
- Keep in regular contact with your customers.
- Create incentives, programs and events to reward customers.
- Let your customers know you appreciate them.
- Always give customers that extra effort.

Index